Revealing The Untold

Published by Gjini Publishing, LLC

www.gjinipublishing.com

Dedication

In loving memory of my beloved sister,
Zibo, who will be forever in my heart.

And to my beloved mother, Kushulla,
who was a loving, caring, and inspiring person.

Acknowledgments

Revealing the Untold began in 2006, when I recorded my life story into small cassettes for my children to have and for them to share it with my future grandchildren. My father never got the chance to tell my children his life story or mine so I knew I had to. After finishing the recording my children encouraged me to share my life story with everyone around the world.

It has been extremely difficult and very emotional for me to bring back the memories of the early years of my life. My family and friends offered inspiration, strength, and their valuable time in listening the cassettes, reading drafts, editing, and conveying ideas.

I would like to express my profound gratitude to my children Erisa and Albi who devoted hours of their precious time during the project. I am grateful to them for their patience, brilliant suggestions, continuous encouragement and their passionate support. This book would not have been written if it had not been for their love and support.

I would like to thank Robin an award-winning Creative Director & Designer from My Custom Book Cover. Her valuable ideas and expertise has been incredible and is greatly appreciated.

I wish to acknowledge the assistance provided by Will and Angelica, students of Brown University, who became an extra set of eyes on my second draft. My gratitude extends to both of them for their time, their honesty, and their suggestions.

My special thanks are extended to my wife who went through many long night of writing, and creativity. I am grateful for her continued support, determination, and leadership throughout the writing of the book.

It has been a pleasure to work closely with all of them. I am grateful for the moments I shared with them, their dedication, and their kindness.

Introduction 7

An End Without Beginning 9

Living on The Brink of Starvation 17

Coping With Year-round Obstacles 25

A Mother's Importance 35

Our Only Asset Is Taken Away 44

New Found Interests 53

Never-Ending Agony 66

Dissatisfaction Builds 79

Mandatory Service 101

One Step Closer 120

Temporary Disappointment 138

Acting Beyond Measures 168

Conflict of the Mind 190

The First Signs of Freedom 213

Finding what was lost 251

Freedom I Once Only Dreamed Of 262

About the Author 270

INTRODUCTION

"Either write something worth reading or do something worth writing."—Benjamin Franklin

My name is Vladimir Gjini, born on September 23rd, 1962 in Albania. Jonuz (my father) and Kushulla (my mother) were highly honored parents of four children of which I am the youngest of four siblings'. My eldest brother, Bedri, was already 10 years old when I was born, and my sister, Zibo, was six. She died in 1978, at the age of 22. Her story comes later. My other sister, Flutra, was two years old. From very early on, an intense desire to learn more about my heritage possessed me. As a child, I heard that a person's name determined his or her nature. That's why I was inspired to conduct research about the true meaning of my name. I discovered that Vladimir came from the Slavic element vladeti, "to rule," combined with meru, meaning "great" or "famous." The second element has also been associated with miru, meaning "peace."

This is the true story of my life in Albania and how I ultimately succeeded in escaping from the clutches of the communist stronghold in my country. My story began in 1969, the year I lost my father. Although I don't remember much of my father's life, the memories I have are marked with a deep sense of fondness and respect for him. As a child, I was no different from most boys who idolized their father. My father—whether he knew it or not—set in motion an unimaginable series of events that transformed my childhood. It was with him that all my pain began, and with whom I became thoroughly acquainted with suffering.

My father's untimely passing changed my life in such profound ways that words cannot adequately communicate the torrent of a nightmarish existence that I inherited. This is my story.

AN END WITHOUT BEGINNING

"If you look up in the night sky he is the only one you see. On a bright day he guides my way. On a quiet night he shines my soul. He is not just any star, he is my star."—Erisa Gjini

In 1969 my world turned as black as night. My heart could see no other color but black; pitch black-pure darkness. Let me just rewind back a few months from this devastating day. As it is extremely difficult to recall memories of my father since I was very young, there are two distinct memories that have been forever engraved into my mind. One being very delightful, and the other being such that no child should ever have to experience.

My earliest and happiest memory of my father was a few months before my entire world came crashing down. My father was a kind, honest, and hardworking man. He would awake early every morning for work and he would return home very late and extremely exhausted. The extreme weather and lack of proper attire made his job more difficult and more challenging than it should have been.

One night, it had been well past my bedtime and I had fallen asleep on the thin, worn out, itchy straw and corn leaf mattress my mother had made for me. I was awoken by a hand gently patting my aching back; shaking me ever so slightly. My eyes peeled open slowly as I was beyond tired from the day's activities. I noticed it was my father. Immediately I sprung up to my feet to give him a hug and kiss as I hadn't seen him all day. He had a smile on his face as he guided me to our fireplace. There he picked up an object of which I could see only a shadow at the moment.

As he brought the object closer into view, I noticed it was a brand new pair of shoes. My soul filled with joy. It was a moment I would never forget. I was so incredibly excited that my smile stretched from ear to ear. It was clear that my entire being was overjoyed for my new pair of shoes father had bought me. I looked up at his tired face and I saw something that made my soul even happier than anything-a smile. A genuine smile from my father as he witnessed his youngest son's soul fill with excitement and whose eyes sparkle at the view of new shoes.

Young Vladimir

My father was fully aware of the hardships and sacrifices he had made to bring home a new pair of shoes for me, but the joy on my face alleviated all the thoughts of hardship he had endured. We both stood there in pure bliss. I was so young I felt like I could run faster and conquer the entire world in my new shoes. For a few moments we stood there silently smiling at each other, perhaps for different reasons, yet the same reason all at the same time, he reached to embrace me and told me that he loved me.

Soon after we broke the embrace my father went to eat and replenish his tired body from a full day of hard work. I knew that was my cue to go back to bed, but the excitement that had just built up in me wouldn't allow me to fall back to sleep. My adrenaline was in full force at that point, so I decided to stay up with my father as he ate his late night dinner. We talked a little and smiled a lot from the excitement. When he was finished with his dinner he tucked me into bed.

As I lay in my bed I thought of how thankful I was for those new shoes. It was so difficult to get a hold of a new pair of shoes considering that our household income was low.

Since it was incredibly rare to receive new shoes as we often received a new pair once every three to four years. We would get shoes that were several sizes larger than our current size, to grow into for the next few years. Knowing all this made me feel blessed and special to have the new pair of shoes.

My great excitement from my new shoes would soon disappear, and my smile would fade into tears rolling down my face. My father bringing home new shoes for me is my only memory of him before the day of darkness occurred. Let me just fast forward to that day.

This was the day that would not only lead to my downfall, but my entire family's, too. The day that I saw my father's eyes fill with a salty, glossy liquid we all call tears, but they were far more than just regular tears. These were little droplets of pain and heartache knowing this father was never going to see the face of his beautiful young son again.

My father, Jonuz Gjini

I remember so vividly the day my father left to go seek whatever medical attention was available at the hospital to treat his asthma. He developed asthma after working outdoors under extreme weather conditions for many years. Unfortunately, the same medications that were used to treat his asthma also increased his risk of myocardial infarction and stroke. As a result of these conditions he was admitted into a hospital multiple times. It was extremely painful to watch each time he was hospitalized.

We could never be sure if he'd make it back home alive; if this would be the last time we see him walking and interacting with life. I always said a little prayer as he left, but this time it was different. I stood there just a few feet away from him balling my eyes out.

This wasn't the first time he had left to go to the hospital, but this was the first and sadly last time he cried hysterically while walking down the stairs to go. He would look ahead, take one step down and then slowly turn his head back toward me. He stared me right in the eyes and I stared right back. I felt the salty tears roll down my cheeks as if they would never end-one droplet after another.

As he would turn to look at me again I could see the pain and sadness take over his entire being. It was all so clear in all the emotions in his face he knew this was most likely going to be the last time he was going to see me. I looked him in the eye and saw the tears streaming down his face.

He didn't say a word to me as he just tried so hard to catch his breath from crying. It was almost as if he and his soul were crying at the same time. It was as if he was unable to control the tears and each teardrop represented the extreme fear of never being able to see me again, never being able to meet my beautiful future wife, never being able to see his own grandchildren and tell them stories of what my life was like when I was younger.

I was so frightened, but I almost tried to convince myself that everything would turn out just fine. No matter how hard I tried there was that gut feeling, after seeing him cry with deep sadness and fear for the first time, that something was seriously wrong. My stomach was turning and I felt like every organ in my body tied into a huge knot. I felt frozen. I knew my dad inching down the stairs was my dad inching away from my life slowly, yet far too quickly.

In October 1969 all my lights turned off. I was left in the pure pitch darkness. My father's soul left me and I felt as if his soul was being torn out of my body piece by piece. I watched as my mother mourned his death. I watched it eat at her each day a little more than the day before. This dark cloud of sadness came over my entire family, but for some reason that cloud trapped my mother. She fell into a deep depression.

LIVING ON THE BRINK OF STARVATION

"Poverty contributes to your strength and wisdom."——Albi Gjini

During this time Albania was under communist rule; this meant that the only person working was the man of the house. In our tragic case the man of the house was no longer with us, and our reality of him had faded into dust. His memory lived in our heads and in our hearts forevermore, but his physical presence was gone. In turn his income was gone as well. As his income was gone this implied that my family was left to starve to death.

The financial crisis we once thought were challenging when my father was alive turned out to be a blessing for us. We were far worse after he was gone. It was in that moment we all realized that the income loss was another reason for my mother's severe depression. As time passed, we (the children) were not the only ones to notice the situation our family was in and the direction we were headed. That direction was south and very dark.

With my family in dire financial straits, my maternal uncle attempted to alleviate our burdens by placing my youngest sister and me into an orphanage. My mother immediately refused, but my uncle, knowing she was unable to take care of us, proceeded with his plan. Fortunately (and for reasons unknown), we were not accepted into the orphanage. Undaunted, he attempted to separate us by sending my youngest sister and me to live with a different relative.

Once again his plan failed as my mother refused to lose us. As a mother she did not want to lose her children under any circumstances. She had already lost the love of her life and she knew she was not going to let anything or anyone come between her and her children. My mother wouldn't approve being separated in any way from her beloved children. She didn't take in my uncle's second attempt at an alternate lifestyle. This was when she knew that she needed to act in order to keep those who were near and dear to her heart living, breathing, and healthy.

*The Gjini family following my father's death: Bedri (my brother, top left);
Kushulla (my mother, top right); Vladimir (me; bottom left);
Flutura (my sister, center); Zibo (my eldest sister, far right)*

Although she had a rough time keeping us happy
as we all continued to mourn the loss of our father, she
wanted to at least know we would sleep with food in our
stomach. My mother went on a hunt for a job.
Thankfully, our situation began to improve when one of

our neighbors offered us help. He was the principal of a local technical school which specialized in educational training. With his recommendation my mother became a janitor at his school.

Finally, we could at least expect a steady source of income every two weeks. I don't know how much she earned once she started working, but it couldn't have been much. Because she was a widow, we became eligible for 400 lek (equal to approximately six U.S dollars at the time) a month per child in government assistance. Even so, things were incredibly difficult for my family.

I remember my mother would leave early in the morning each day and she would come home late at night. Frequently my siblings and I would stay over at my neighbor's house until she arrived home. Our neighbor, a sweet elderly woman, offered to keep us in her house while our mother wasn't home. She had a heart of gold. As soon as my mother came home from work she would pick us up and bring us to our own house.

My mother would feed us and then sit down after a long day of work. After she had her short rest she would get up to eat a slice of bread, which was considered her dinner. She would then come over to us, tuck us into bed, and later would fall asleep herself. We all were able to notice that she wasn't her usual self. She was progressively becoming more and more depressed.

A black cloud had taken over her mind and body. I would later find out another cause for her depression. As she was working at the school as a janitor the students there would make fun of her straight to her face. It wasn't common for women to have a job in Albania at the time. Not only was it uncommon, but it was even less common for a woman to have a position as a school's janitor.

During this time I had no idea that these people were making fun of my heart-broken mother because she never expressed it. The day I found out that these cruel students were making fun of her my heart sunk from my chest straight to my toes and hit the floor so hard it shattered into millions of small pieces. Knowing what she was going through and having people hurt her even more emotionally made me feel disgusted.

My mother tried her best to ease our difficult lives. Even so, sometimes it was impossible. Living a life where breakfast and lunch were considered one meal was so rough. All we could afford was bread, so it comprised the majority of our diet. For breakfast, my mother would often make papare, which is just bread softened in hot water. She would drain the water and add a tablespoon or two of oil mixed with a bit of red pepper. Other mornings, she would make trahana, which is similar to oatmeal. She boiled trahana, adding bread and oil to enhance the taste.

Sometimes, breakfast consisted of one slice of bread with a small amount of sugar and olive oil. This single slice of bread would have to last us the entire morning and the entire afternoon. All I could remember was my stomach constantly growling. The thought of going the entire day without anything more than a single slice of bread made me so depressed. My stomach would ache for days upon days, and there was nothing that I or my mother could do about it. I could tell by the look on her face that it hurt her far worse than it hurt us; to see us not eating a proper diet due to a shortage of income.

My mother tried everything in her power to make sure we ate and it was somewhat tasty. I was honestly so grateful every time I saw the food. My eyes would sparkle and my face would light up at the sight of the food. I knew that I would be able to get through my day with something in my stomach.

Most days I would only eat once, which was considered my breakfast, lunch, and dinner because we were far too poor to afford separate meals for each time of day. My friends would ask me which was my favorite breakfast and I would honestly not have an answer. As long as I knew I was eating I was enjoying my food no matter what it was. The thought of being able to eat was enough to satisfy not only hunger and happiness, but also my taste buds.

Dinner almost always included watery soup. To stretch the soup, my mother would add a lot of water and serve it with bread. Only a small amount of bread, though – she had to save the rest for next morning's breakfast. On very rare occasions we would have rice or spaghetti for dinner.

Always thinking of her children first, my mother regularly starved herself knowing that her paycheck and the government assistance was not enough to last two weeks. Oftentimes, there was only enough food for 11 or 12 days between paychecks, so we would go hungry for the next two or three days. On those nights, the wood floor felt even colder and less inviting. Although there were no rugs or coverings on the floor it was seldom (if ever) dusty. My mother was a neat freak (perhaps to the point of an obsessive-compulsive cleaner).

Often, I would spend all night trying to find a position in which the floor didn't grind against my achy bones – that, and listening sniffles near my feet. It was a sound that I came to know all too well. It was the sound of my mother, weeping at the thought of having to lay her unfed children to sleep on a hardwood floor.

Every day, I ate very small portions to conserve food for the next. Each meager meal left me even hungrier. As I walked back from school, the smell of food wafted out of my neighbors' windows. The smell made my stomach ache unbearably. Starving and malnourished, I constantly felt dizzy, sometimes to the point of nearly collapsing. Incessant hunger pains essentially sucked any happiness out of my childhood.

On one occasion, my grandmother came to visit and she was horrified by my condition: emaciated, exhausted, and stricken with jaundice. After learning from my mother that it had been almost a week since my last meal, she took me to one of my neighbors, who took pity on me and relinquished a piece of bread and a cup of milk. I devoured the food and experienced a terrible stomachache in return.

COPING WITH YEAR-ROUND OBSTACLES

"That which does not kill us makes us stronger."—
Friedrich Nietzsche

During the late spring, we planted tomatoes, cucumbers, peppers, eggplants, onions, garlic, and string beans. In the summer, the soup was a lot heartier, filled with whatever vegetables we could find in our garden. The vegetables that grew in the garden were of critical importance to my family, and we often pickled tomatoes and eggplants for use in the winter. We also dried the onions and garlic for future use, as well as the September figs that grew on our garden's sole tree.

In the summer, we tried to save some money wherever we could because we needed money for schoolbooks – books which cost approximately 600 lek per child. Even so, we could never save enough. Often, I would purchase used books from older children, even if they were in terrible condition. Sometimes, I would just have to attend classes without them, hoping that other students would share theirs with me. We simply did not have enough money to afford the basic supplies for

school, such as notebooks and pencils. I was constantly
borrowing from my friends.

After September, we had to prepare for the cold
weather. On weekends, I had to go into the village to
gather chestnuts for the government, while my mother
stayed at home and knit our sweaters. This was also the
best time to visit my grandmother and my uncle who
lived in Prongji. I lived in the city, and every time I went
to the village I would purchase two loaves of wheat
bread to bring to my grandmother. For them, wheat
bread – which they normally weren't allowed to have –
was very special. They ate only cornbread, which felt
like sand in the mouth when it was cold and stale.

I had to gather a certain amount of chestnuts to
get three kilograms in return (this was my pay). My
uncle was a shepherd, so my grandmother would get
wool from his sheep and hide it for us. With seven
children of his own, it was very difficult for him to help
us. Every time I left my grandmother's house, she would
put corn and wool in my chestnut bag. The wool was for
my mom to knit the sweaters for us.

Unfortunately, the wool was never enough for
all of us to have new sweaters each year, so my mother
would undo the good parts of old sweaters, thread the

wool again and knit a new sweater with it. One year, none of us had sweaters to pass the winter. I remember my mother making the comforters herself and stuffing them with old pieces of cloth.

When my mother first got married, my grandmother made her a comforter stuffed with wool as a special gift. That winter, she ripped that comforter apart and pulled out the wool to make sweaters for us. That was the only year that all of us had new sweaters for the winter.

Because money was so scarce, we couldn't afford to buy winter coats. Most years, I would have to endure the winter without a coat, and with leaky shoes that were coming apart from overuse. I remember constantly having cold, wet feet at school during winter months.

As much as we tried to prepare, we were never ready for winter. Typically, food saved from the summer was used up by December. Once that was gone, we bought just enough food to survive. Sometimes we went to our neighbors with a small Turkish coffee cup and borrow some salt or sugar.

Generating heat was another constant challenge. The only source of practical heat came from burning wood, which we had to purchase for approximately 500 lek per month. Many times my family went through the winter months without heat, and when we did have wood, only one room could be heated for a few hours in the evening. Even when I was in elementary school, I would have to go home and chop wood into thinner pieces, so it would fit in our stove.

We had an old-fashioned stove which only used wood, with pipes going around the room to release the smoke outside. On windy days, the smoke would be blown back into the room, which meant we had to open the windows to clear the air. We quickly learned to make the most of what we had. Since there were no washers and dryers in Albania, my mom had to wash clothes by hand during the day and dry them on warm pipes at night.

We didn't have electricity every night, either. Sometimes the government cut off power to homes whenever there wasn't enough to supply the rest of the country—or when we couldn't afford to pay the bill. On those nights, my mother would make a makeshift candle with a jar, oil, and some cloth. Some nights, that was the only source of light. Unfortunately, the thick smoke it let off covered everything in the house, from the walls to our noses.

The rainy, snowy and windy days were the worst for us. Desperately in need of repair, our house was old and without any insulation. Whenever it rained the ceiling leaked. Whenever the wind blew hard, we felt it inside. Many nights, we woke up from the rain dripping onto our comforters or even our faces. We had to use empty pails, pots, and pans to collect the water. If we overslept and forgot to empty them, we'd wake up to a flooded room. Our beds were really just straw mats, so a wet floor meant wet mats and wet comforters. The following night we didn't have covers, we would have to use those wet comforters as mattresses—I remember lying awake till morning, shaking violently from the cold.

Taking showers was another major issue during winter months. Often, one shower a week was all we could have. Things were constantly in short supply, including water and soap. For us, shampoo and laundry detergent didn't even exist. Most families were limited to buying five soaps a month. Regardless of the number of family members, Albanians had to figure a way to make five soaps last for cleaning dishes, washing clothes, and taking showers. I often gathered sticks so my mother would boil the white clothes in a big pot outside. In place of soap, she used the ash of the wood.

My hometown was called Gjirokaster. It was a beautiful place, but bitterly cold in the winter. Gjirokaster was built on the face of Mount Mali I Gjere —one of three mountains forming a "U" shape. The other mountains are Mali Cajupi to the east and Mali Bureto to the south. The north side is wide open, letting the winds through.

However, no amount of scenic beauty could make life easier for the families in our town. Even families that had some money couldn't purchase many necessities because they simply weren't available. There were few stores downtown, and only one store per neighborhood. Essentially, Albania didn't have enough food to feed everyone. The government assigned each family a maximum amount of foods to purchase.

Each family was assigned two kilograms of flour, one liter of vegetable oil, 1/2 liter of olive oil, 1 ½ pounds of feta cheese, three packs of spaghetti, one pack of fresh coffee beans, and one kilogram of sugar per month. The availability of produce varied throughout the year. Families with money often lined up around 2 AM for a chance to buy milk that was delivered at 6:30 AM. Our family was too poor to buy milk every day; rather, we bought milk every seven to 10 days. However, they did give priority to the families that had babies. The rest of the families could only hope to buy milk, because there was no guarantee any would be available when they finally made it to the front of the line.

During the holiday season the availability of food in stores was greater. During Christmas and other religious holidays, every family bought and cooked something extra. Parents never told the children the reason why: they didn't want the children to talk with their friends about religion. In 1967, the Albanian government forbade its people to practice religion, talk about religion, or pray openly. If children talked about religion outside their homes, their parents could end up in prison for the rest of their lives.

Each New Year's, most families in Albania received a small present. The companies would withhold a small amount out of the payroll of their workers to use for a raffle. The presents included small balls, toy cars, plastic dolls, and things of the sort. We generally didn't have toys to play with, so we had to make our own. Often we would play with sticks and rocks, and other times we would make makeshift soccer balls out of tied cloth. For us boys, balls of any sort were the most exciting gifts. We played soccer with them until they ripped beyond recognition. Many times, we would try to repair them so we could continue to play soccer.

In Albania, there was no snow removal equipment, so snow could stay on the ground for long periods of time. A few days of snow created layer upon layer of ice, making foot travel dangerous. Children, on the other hand, had a lot of fun with the snow. Like other children around the world, we had snowball fights and made a snowman. Because winters were long, we had to think of creative ways to play with the snow. To catch birds, we would place a stick in the snow, tie a string to it and a cardboard box, and position the stick on a slant.

Then we left some food close to the box for birds to eat, and waited. When a bird came to get the food we pulled the string to trap it. When we succeeded, we would take the bird home, feed it, play with it for a little, but always release it afterwards.

In the spring, the warmth of the sun was very pleasing– it felt like a blanket covering my whole body. Even as a child, however, spring marked the beginning of hard labor. After my father's death, my older brother (who was seventeen at the time) became angry and bitter – and quickly lost control of his life. He stopped going to school, and he was never home either. As a result, from a very young age, I had the responsibility of overseeing our house, making sure everything that needed to get done got done. After school, I had to collect manure for our backyard while my mother collected green leaves for cooking. After I had collected enough manure, I had to flip dirt with a shovel, and then mix them together into compost.

When I was younger, my grandmother used to plant the vegetable seeds for us. However, starting that year, I went into the village, picked up the seeds, and started doing it myself. During the early summer, I would collect leaves from a certain plant, dry them, and sell them as medicinal herbs. There was a special place I could go and drop the leaves off, where they would inspect them. It was a lot of work to collect one kilogram of dry leaves, but doing so helped the family a little – so I did it.

Years of hard work, living in squalor, and watching her children starve greatly exacerbated my mother's depression. While I did work outside, my older sister had to take over the responsibilities inside the house. For a long time, my mom took antidepressant medications without food. Doing this destroyed her stomach lining, and she was constantly wracked with intense pain. As a result of the unbearable pain she stopped taking the antidepressant and her condition got worse.

A MOTHER'S IMPORTANCE

"We expect everything and are prepared for nothing."——Anne Sophie Swetchine

In the span of three or four years, my mother was hospitalized three times. The first time she remained in the hospital for a month. Each time she was admitted, the duration of her stay increased. One morning I woke up to the sound of my doorbell ringing. I was very cranky, my entire body was so incredibly sore, and achy from the prior day's workload in the intense heat.

I was never able to get enough rest as it was, but the doorbell awakening me just as I was sleeping had eliminated even more sleep from my day. After moments of feeling cranky I began to come to my senses and wake up a bit more to realize I was the man of the house now. I needed to make sure who it was at my door, so I slowly forced myself to sit up and then eventually stand up and make my way to the door.

As I walked past my ill mother I noticed she was not doing very well. Her face was pale; her body looked weak; her eyes looked sad and tired; and her hair was a mess. It was as if her messy hair resembled the mess her life had become ever since my father had left us. She was leaning on our kitchen table hardly balancing herself. Immediately my heart dropped to my stomach.

In that very moment I knew who was going to be at the door; what was going to happen; what was wrong with my beloved ill mother; where she would end up going; what I was about to witness; and how the next hour would go down. The sadness immediately overflowed within me as I approached our door. I saw the face I was expecting to see. I looked up at my uncle eagerly waiting by the gate with a look on his face that could tell it all. It was a look like he knew what he would have to go through and do. He seemed like he was used to this kind of thing.

I approached the gate and let my uncle in. As he quickly walked straight past me and immediately toward the area where my mother always stayed I looked ahead near the gate and saw the ambulance awaiting my mother's arrival. Tears began to form in my eyes at the sight of confirmation. The sight of my uncle was the first confirmation of what I was going through was correct and the ambulance parked outside the metal gate was the second and final confirmation of my thoughts.

A piece of my heart broke a little each time this would happen. I knew this feeling all too well. I knew I needed to remain strong in my mother's eyes for the time being and I would have the opportunity to express my sad emotions afterwards. After what seemed to be gut-wrenching hours of pain standing at the door in confirmation I snapped myself back to reality.

I walked my way back to the room where my mother had been resting; where my uncle was now headed. I saw him gently look her in the eyes; slowly wrap his fingers around her fragile little arm; telling her that she needed this, and she must follow him. This was not the first time that my mom was being escorted to treat her depression. We've all seen this before. My uncle began to slightly pull her fragile body toward the door and she immediately refused.

She didn't want to leave her four children; to her, that was more painful than any physical pain she could ever endure. It was as though her depressive state had reached its climax as a single teardrop fell from her big, brown eye. As I watched the tear roll down her cheek, she looked over at me with sadness in her gaze.

She tried her hardest to fight against my uncle's attempt to bring her to the ambulance, but he was much stronger. He eventually brought her to the ambulance doors and she kept looking back at me; crying. She kept refusing to enter the ambulance and leave her beautiful young children alone. My uncle lifted her to the ambulance door and I saw her hands grasp onto the outside edges of the door. Her fingertips pressed firmly against the edges of the door and she wept for minutes more, still refusing to enter.

I knew she needed to go and as much as it tore at my heartstrings to have to not only see her going through heartache, but also have her leave to the hospital. I knew it was for her benefit and ultimately for ours as well. I pulled myself together and approached her desperate being. I looked her directly in the eye and I reached up with my hand, as I was so small I couldn't reach, and she bent down close to my face. I looked her in the eye and I felt my eyes begin to water.

My heart felt so heavy and my breathing rapidly increased. I brushed my small finger across her cheek and wiped away a single tear. I watched that tear fall to the ground with a splash, spread apart, and shattered when it hit the ground. My heart did the same thing. As the tear was falling through the air, waiting to hit the ground, I felt my heart sink toward the ground waiting to burst into a million and one pieces.

She whispered to me, "I love you" and I let a tear fall and kissed her cheek. I told her that if she loved me she would go to the hospital for me and come back home stronger and healthier. This broke her heart to hear I could see it in her upset face. She kissed my forehead and I told her that we would be perfectly fine, and she had absolutely not a thing in the world to worry about except getting herself better.

We stared into each other's souls for a short while, and in sync we both let our last tear roll down our cheeks, she kissed me, and stood up again. I grabbed her hand, as it was the only part of her I could reach, I pressed my lips against the back of her hand, looked up to her, and said, "I love you, mami". At that moment she let go of the other edge of the door and walked into the ambulance.

I watched as my uncle filed into the ambulance right behind my beautiful mother. I then watched as they closed the ambulance door. I slowly made my way to the door of the house and walked in. I inched my way to the same spot my beloved mother once stood. That very moment was when I let the waterworks flow. It was like a river with no end. I must have sat there for hours balling my eyes out. My siblings would pass by me, see me crying and once every now and then tried to comfort me.

However, they were emotional and just as unstable as I was, therefore, they didn't know many comforting words. As the night approached we all laid down for bed lined up next to each other on our straw mattresses. None of us said a single word. It was pure silence and we all just laid there staring at the ceiling, letting all the tears hit from our eyes onto the mattresses.

As the next morning began to approach and the sun began to peek through the window I woke up. It felt weird to open my eyes and wake up. I didn't remember falling asleep. All I remembered was my mind racing, thoughts-good and bad-flowing in and out of my mind, while tears spilled from my eyes; not to mention the massive headache I was experiencing. I got up to get a glass of water when I heard the front door open.

It startled me at first, but then I realized it was just my uncle. He saw me near tears and we stared each other in the eyes for a few seconds, and he just wrapped his arms around me. He held me so tight and whispered in my ear "it's all going to be okay; she's going to be back home in no time." He held me for a little bit longer and kissed the top of my head and left to go comfort my siblings.

I grabbed my glass of water and tried to swallow it along with the huge lump in my throat. I turned to walk to the area where my uncle and siblings were, but as I turned I bumped into my uncle. He walked past me, pulled out a chair from under the kitchen table, and sat on it. He pulled me by my waist and sat me on his lap. He dragged his index finger across my cheek and wiped past my teardrop and turned my head to face him. He grabbed my small hand and interlocked our fingers and with his calloused thumb he rubbed the back of my hand. I knew I was in good and safe hands, but I also couldn't fathom the thought of my sickly mother present in my thoughts.

The first time my mother was admitted to the hospital I was still very young. While she remained in the hospital I lived with my uncle in the village for a month. In his village the children woke up early— around 4 AM—to gather tobacco leaves. Before going to school, they had to help their families. I joined them, hoping the extra money would help my uncle. In return, my uncle brought me to the school in the village. I couldn't survive more than a day there.

As soon as I arrived, the students started making fun of me – calling me an orphan, and saying that my mother was crazy. It was incredibly painful to live without a father figure when I was young and not having a mother around was devastating also. I couldn't bear to hear their cruelty, so I ended up missing the entire month of school. Once the month passed I could finally go back home and reunite with my family. Even though I had nothing to eat at home, and one of the walls of our house was falling apart, I was extremely excited to return.

We desperately needed to repair our house but no one was willing to extend credit to our family. One of our neighbors – a corrupt director of a clothing company – was married but secretly kept a mistress on the side. To mask his actions he needed a house for this woman to live in – so he planned to take ours. Since my father was dead and my mother ill, my 17-year old brother had to sign the documents and make decisions for the household. Knowing this, our neighbor offered to help us with renovations. My brother noticed his true intentions and refused to sign the documents. To circumvent my brother's resistance my neighbor used his influence to draft my brother into the army just before the legal age. Therefore, before he was even 18 (in communist Albania, it was mandatory for all boys to serve once they turned 18) my brother found himself serving in the army.

OUR ONLY ASSET IS TAKEN AWAY

"Tricks and treachery are the practice of fools, that don't have brains enough to be honest."—Benjamin Franklin

Now that my brother was out of the way, my neighbor joined forces with our uncle, who quickly signed the necessary papers to start construction on our home. With my brother gone, my neighbor started construction on our house, which took two and a half years to complete. We had to move to a house across the street, which had only one room – and a bathroom shared with two other families.

We had to pay rent for this apartment, which caused our financial situation to worsen even further. We started borrowing money from our uncles and neighbors, and my older sister, who was in eighth grade at the time, decided to quit school and look for a job.

It was difficult to find a job in Albania, since essentially all available jobs were managed from the borough hall. Nobody knew what jobs were available unless they worked for or had some connection with the borough hall. In practice, all the jobs were going under the table to communist families, while anticommunist families were severely discriminated against.

After a long search, my sister found a job as a tailor's assistant – a position which was a 35-minute walk from our home. From noon until 3:00 PM the workplace was closed. Every day she left the house early in the morning, came home at break time, and went back until the evening. During the winter months I went to pick her up from work. Every night, I waited outside by the door for her because she was afraid to walk home alone in the dark.

Deep down inside, however, I knew I could be of no help if something were to actually happen. I was too young to protect her. When her co-workers saw me waiting outside in the cold, they would let me come inside. The place was filled with beautiful new clothes – it was overwhelming; I felt like I didn't belong there. Every time I stepped in, I became aware of how old and raggedy my clothes were, and I felt a sense of shame – so much so that I preferred to wait outside in the cold.

Her income wasn't much, either, but it helped a great deal. We still lived in poverty, but at least now we could pay our rent. Little by little, we began to pay off our other debts. I was very young, but every day after school I went to help the workers renovating our old house. When the ground was wet, the delivery truck couldn't make it up the hill where the house was located, so I would help the workers to carry the materials. Carrying the heavy materials uphill made my legs shake and my arms burn, but more than anything I wanted the construction to finish as soon as possible. However, the workers took their time and later I learned that they wanted to claim more money on the renovation. I just loved my old house and I couldn't stay away from it much longer.

On weekends I played there with my friends. One rainy Sunday we were playing tag. The third floor wasn't finished yet; therefore, studs and beams were all around. I was standing on top of a pile of sand, looking out for my friend. When he ran to tag me I started running on the beams to avoid him catching me. My foot slipped and I fell to the second floor, causing my head to hit a sharp rock.

I was knocked unconscious and seriously injured. All I remember is going in and out of conscious few times, but later I learned that my friends picked me up and carried me to the main clinic 40 minutes away. They didn't have a phone to notify the clinic and there was no transportation available to transport me there. As soon as the doctor saw my condition he applied some pressure to the laceration to stop bleeding, and called an ambulance to transport me to a hospital to treat my injury. I was discharged around 11:30 PM that night. They drove me home from the hospital in an ambulance, but I refused for them to drop me off by my house. My family didn't know anything about it, and, as a child, I was scared that they would be angry with me.

Thinking that they would be sleeping, I wanted to slip into bed unnoticed and act like nothing had happened the next day. In reality, they were incredibly worried and had been searching through the neighborhood for hours. When I was walking toward the house, my older sister saw my head wrapped with gauze. I was expecting her to yell at me; instead, she hugged me and showered me with kisses. Instead of bringing me home, she sent me to my next door neighbor: she didn't want my mother to see me in that condition.

I later learned that during the search, my mother had been crying hysterically and her condition had worsened. My sister went inside, told her that I had been found, calmed her down, and waited for her to fall asleep. Afterwards, she took me home and tucked me in.

My mother cried when she saw me the next morning. I never told her about the hospital or what had really happened. Even though I was in severe pain, I told her that I was fine, that it was just a little scratch. As soon as I had recovered, I went back to help the workers.

When construction on the house was complete the communists had accomplished their goal. Before the construction started, the initial plan was for us to pay mortgage. With our income, that was inconceivable. We agreed to rent only one level of the house, and that was going to be our way of paying the mortgage. Instead, they took over our house. They rented the third floor to us and his mistress' family and they made us pay rent to them. They rented the second floor to another family who had seven children and opened a daycare on the first floor.

Having a daycare in our house wasn't helpful for my mother's condition. My mother couldn't handle all that noise every day. At home, she was disturbed by the noise that the children made. At work, she was disturbed by the students making fun of her for being ill. My grandmother tried very hard and was determined to get my mother on disability benefits. For months, my grandmother went from office to office. She met many different people and tried to explain our situation and my mother's condition so they would let her go on disability. In Albania, there was a lot of corruption and bureaucracy. It was very difficult for someone to receive disability benefits even if the individual met all the requirements for it. My grandmother insisted for a long time - and, eventually, my mother was qualified to receive what she had deserved long ago.

I was very happy when I heard the news. She was a smart, loving, and caring mother. Suffering from severe depression didn't mean that she was crazy or careless; I was devastated when people thought of her in such a way. My mother started to collect 3,800 lek (approximately $54.00 at the time) in disability benefits every month. Between my mother's benefits and my sister's income we thought we were going to be okay.

Shortly after, my brother was released from the army. At first, he was responsible and he came home every night. It didn't last long, though. Gradually, he went back to not coming home for days, and sometimes for months. He hurt our family a lot. On days that my mother had to go and collect the disability benefits he went to meet her there. She was so happy to see him. My brother would ask my mother for some money and disappear again.

That was a big problem for my family because we didn't have enough money to get by. My older sister didn't want him in the house anymore because of what he was doing, which was very difficult to process as a young boy. They started fighting about the money. Sometimes when I walked back from school with my friends, I could hear them fighting from the street. I felt embarrassed in front of my friends, but I pretended that I didn't hear anything and that nothing was happening.

As soon as my friends were past the courtyard I ran up the steps to my home. I tried to tell them to stop fighting. My brother was stronger and hit her during their fights. Sometimes, I saw my sister holding an object to protect herself. These moments terrified me. I loved both of my siblings and was afraid they would seriously hurt each other. I tried to get in the middle to separate them, begging them not to fight. I didn't want my brother to leave, but in those moments that's exactly what I told him to do. I realized that the longer he stayed, the more the fighting would escalate. And it was already dangerous. I was crying and very sad to see him leave, but it was the best option for all of us.

This situation didn't help my mother's illness and I did my best to comfort her. I went close to my mother and gave her a hug and a kiss. We were both shaking. When my siblings fought, my mother couldn't do anything but cry because it was dangerous to get in between them. My brother should have been the one to lead my family; instead, he caused more problems.

Time passed, and my brother eventually calmed down. He found a job, had his own private life, and no longer sought us out for money. He didn't help the family financially, but at least he started coming home and improved greatly. A few years later he got married and his life changed even more. They lived with us and a few months after the wedding his wife gave birth to a baby boy named Emiliano.

I got along with my sister-in-law very well. I treated her like my sister and we had a great relationship. Four years after their first child, they had another boy, named Ilirian. A couple of years later they had the third child, whom they named Jonuz, after my father. After her first child, my sister-in-law became ill. Once a month, for about a week, she had seizures every half an hour that lasted few minutes each time. During this time, her tongue blocked her airway and someone had to be

there to make sure of her safety. Her entire body shook
during these episodes.

NEW FOUND INTERESTS

"Watch your thoughts; They become words. Watch your words; They become actions. Watch your actions; They become habits. Watch your habits; They become character. Watch your character: It becomes your destiny."—Lao Tzu

Whenever my sister-in-law had seizures, my brother couldn't go to work in the morning. He had to stay with her until I returned from school to relieve him. My brother taught me what to do to prevent blockage of her airway and how to make sure she was safe during the episodes. Those moments were frightening for me. Watching her suffer so immensely was unbearable. Eventually, she was referred to a specialist who helped to improve her condition.

It was difficult to endure the financial and emotional stresses at home, but that didn't stop me from being intelligent. I was always interested in learning any information that I could. When I was young televisions were not available to Albanians. In the 1960s people owned radios, but TVs came to the Albanian market in the late 70s. Few families could afford to buy one, and even then, few TVs were available on the market. Even the politicians were on waiting lists for TVs. However, the reality of having a TV was not as exciting as one would think. There was only one TV station and it was available only a few hours in the morning and a few hours in the evening.

Even though my family didn't own a TV or radio, I was still exposed to these things through my friends. The movies they played on TV were always tied to politics- communist propaganda. Most movies or shows depicted homelessness in other countries, stressing crimes and violence elsewhere to keep the country brainwashed; to believe that we were in excellent shape; that we had a great government. The communists wanted us to think that they were successful rulers.

Everything in Albania was connected to politics, even in the schools. Once a week, the first period in class was information about news from outside the country. We had to submit articles from the newspapers about wrongdoings that happened around the world. I learned a lot through my friends and school, but I was eager to learn more.

Another way that I learned was through books.
Throughout my childhood I read a lot of books, mostly
written by Mark Dodani. I read "Mysafiri", "Operacioni
Zjarri", "Fronti i Heshtun", "Takim Apo Duel", and
more. Mark Dodani had been an officer in the secret
services of Albania since 1946. He served as an Albanian
agent for thirty-five years. His primary nicknames were
"Xhakoni" and "Studenti". Most importantly, his books
helped me understand from an early age that life outside
the country was different-and even better. His books
revealed the opposite of what we learned in Albania.
What we had learned was that life in other countries was
invariably worse than in Albania, but that wasn't true.
His books made me realize the truth and helped me
develop a different perspective about the real world.

I realized that we were being deceived in
Albania; the citizens were misled and many believed
what they were being told. I realized that the
communists were dictators; that we were all trapped here
by them. All the borders of Albania were closed like a
prison.

Nobody was allowed to cross the borders of
Albania, and it was nearly impossible if somebody
wanted to escape. There was a very high electrified

fence which kept us all in Albania. We had no idea about what other places were actually like, and how could we find out with fences like these? If someone was caught loitering near the borders, they would be incarcerated for the rest of their lives. Many people were caught. The borders were protected very well, and if the soldiers caught someone crossing, they beat them to death or shot them.

It was better to die than to be in their hands. Having grown up with only glimpses of the outside world from books I developed an early desire to escape what was a living nightmare in the remote repressive state of Albania, under the totalitarian rule of Enver Hoxha.

Occasionally, my brother and I stayed up late, talked about the events of our day, and had fun together. On a particularly snowy winter night, my brother told me stories about the army. He served in a town along the border with Yugoslavia. Sometimes they had 5 to 6 feet of snow in that town, and even then they had to stay outside to protect the borders. He told me how they were friendly with Yugoslavian soldiers and how they patrolled the area to maintain security.

After a certain point I asked my brother, "If we wanted to escape, would you know the way?" He answered without hesitation, not understanding how seriously I meant this, "Of course I know. I served there for a long time." Then, I asked what would happen if maybe someday we could escape together. This scared my brother because I was only thirteen, which was very young to feel and express this way. He told me to be quiet, to never speak like that. That was the first time that I verbally expressed how I'd like to leave the country. Even the words were dangerous.

Maybe I was too young to know these details, but the combination of learning through school and media gave me a different perspective on life. I was always eager to learn and I was doing very well, especially in algebra and physics. The teachers called me a genius and never checked my homework. They knew it was done, and it was done correctly. If there were problems other children couldn't understand, the teachers asked me to stand in front of the class and solve it. I could teach them anything.

More than anything, I enjoyed art-I spent all of my free time drawing. When the teachers saw my drawings they suggested that I take art courses after school. The town provided free sessions for children who were talented in the arts, so I started going three times a week for two hours each time. I found that the more time I spent developing my artistic skills the more my love for art grew. My dream was to finish middle school and attend art school in Tirana, the capital of Albania. The only way to be accepted into that school was to win an entrance competition during summer break.

I was very excited and certain that I would secure a spot at this school. On the day of the competition, I left home feeling confident that my dream would come true, but when I arrived I was told that the competition had actually taken place days before and that someone else had won. I was devastated, yet I understood why the government officials administering the competition had given me the wrong date: my father was an anti-communist and everyone knew it.

Before WWII, he was very vocal about his beliefs, but that was before Albania became a communist country. After the war, he knew better than to publicly share his views. He had a family to provide for and if he continued to raise his voice he would be imprisoned for the rest of his life. Unfortunately, I believe that the government still knew about his anti-communist leanings and had purposefully sabotaged me-the son of an anti-communist-by giving me the wrong competition date. Everyone knew I deserved the spot and agreed that it was unfair for them to use this method to sabotage me. Their sympathy was nice, but it wasn't enough to soften the blow.

Not being able to enroll into art school was a huge disappointment for me. I didn't want to continue school anymore. I felt there was no point of continuing my education if I couldn't pursue my dream. All of my teachers from middle school were in shock when they heard about what happened with the art competition. It was a shame whenever the talents of a student were wasted, especially when it was as a result of circumstances the student could not control, such as the political views of a parent. The teachers came to my house multiple times to talk to my family and tried to convince me to continue education; to attend the high school in my town. I simply didn't want to go there.

One day during the summer while playing soccer with my friends we saw a group of teachers coming toward us. We stopped playing and spoke with them for a bit, then they pulled me aside to speak with me privately. Once again, they tried to explain to me how important it was to continue my education because a student like me could succeed, no matter how hard others tried to stop me.

Their determination to make a difference in my life moved me. After that conversation, I promised them that I would attend the high school. That September I started the high school, but it was difficult for me to be even remotely remain interested in my classes.

In my country the board of education decided where everyone attended high school. Students didn't have the right to choose as they do in many other countries. My first cousin, Rashide (Secretary of the Party Committee of the Gjirokaster), was one of the leaders of our town, and I was lucky to learn through her that the board of education had assigned me to attend the shoe and leather technical school in Tirana.

After two years in Tirana, I would have to train for another four years in my hometown. Even though this wasn't my dream, I was still excited to hear about my assignment. At the same time I was devastated. I felt that this was the second time that the board of education had sabotaged my career. It was known that some people paid under the table to ensure their desired assignments.

It turned out that they were going to give my place in the technical school to one of my neighbors-a member of a communist family.

Initially, I found myself at a loss for what to do, but I couldn't allow them to strip me of my happiness twice. That same day, I walked for four hours to get to my uncle's house. I told him that I didn't have time to waste; that if I were not in Tirana by tomorrow my life would take a drastically different direction. The next morning we went to the technical school together.

When we arrived at the principal's office she told us that the first two weeks of school had already passed, and Albanian school rules dictated that if the student failed to show up for the first two weeks, they were automatically expelled from school. I was disqualified. My uncle explained the situation, mentioned that I wasn't notified and that this had already happened to me with the art school, and she made an exception.

I was extremely excited for the exception because I knew that education would help me with job placement in the future. I started school that same day, and after school my uncle and I went to the store. I was grateful for the new clothes he bought me and for his role in securing my place in school. I could not thank him enough. We spent the rest of the evening together and the next morning he went home.

I did well in school, had housing, food, and was moving forward. It was great for me, but not for my family in Gjirokaster. My room and board drained almost half of their income. They started borrowing money again to survive. It pained me to see them so affected by my choices. I was heading in the right direction, but I wasn't happy that my family had to struggle in order to pay for my education. I knew they were willing to make the financial and emotional sacrifice for my education as long as I did well. I definitely made sure that this was the case.

Here I am taking a break while in technical school in Tirana.
It's my first time living apart from my beloved family.

I was doing very well academically and physically. I lived on campus, started eating three meals a day (which was unusual for me), and exercised frequently. I had developed a routine. Every morning around 3:30 I went running with one of my friends. After that, we went on the school's field and exercised some more. By 7:00 AM I was showered and ready to start school. After school, I had to study. Sometimes in the evening, I had free time to spend with my friends. We weren't allowed to leave campus, but we stayed together and had fun. In the winter on campus everyone had to be in their rooms by 7:00 PM because the electricity was shut off almost every night at that time. We weren't even allowed in the hallways. The boys stayed on the second floor and the girls on the third. At least, those were the rules.

Oftentimes, the hallways were full of students when the power was off. For fun, the boys placed a few pails of water in the middle of the hallway. One of them would shout that security was coming to scare other students. Thinking security was actually there, students ran in the dark towards their rooms and tripped on the pails. In the middle of the hallway were a bunch of students in a pile, screaming and cursing because they were hurt and wet. Other times in the afternoon, we went through the rooms to find students napping and paint mustaches or beards on their faces. These weren't appropriate pranks, but we didn't have much to do, so we had to come up with something.

The first year in school went well and in 1978 the second year had just started. I was so excited sitting in class thinking about the fresh start to a new year. I was reminiscing on the past school year and I was filled with feelings of joy. This was a reoccurring feeling up until a few weeks into fall. One afternoon while I was getting ready for the following day, I was called down to the principal's office. I wasn't sure if I would be praised or if I would be in trouble. As I made my way down to her office I slowed my pace, trying to remember all the things I had done during the past week. I was trying to figure out why I was called down. It was so frightening walking to her office not knowing her intentions.

However, I just couldn't seem to think of any wrongdoing. When I entered the office she looked me in the eye and told me to have a seat. It wasn't normal for the principal to ask a student to take a seat. I was so confused. Cautiously, I took a seat and looked at her facial expression. I could tell she was having a difficult time getting whatever was on her mind into words. We both sat in silence for a few moments. As each moment passed each moment seemingly became longer and longer. I sat there shaking on the inside. I knew whatever she was going to say was most definitely going to be bad.

NEVER-ENDING AGONY

"The only time goodbye is painful is when you know you will never say hello again."——Unknown

I felt beads of sweat begin to form on my forehead and on the back of my neck. I clenched my fists, which were so watery and sweaty they slipped apart when I tried to intertwine my fingers and hold one hand in the other. Just as the sweat began to roll down the side of my face I heard the principal speak. She began to say something, but she had no voice. She choked on her words and then she paused, placed her hands on her head, sat there for a few seconds, and finally she said it. She said the words that you watch on TV or hear stories about, but never even think would become your reality.

She told me that my house was burned after catching fire earlier. I was looking at her, but immediately my trance fell to my feet. I looked downward trying to digest what the principal had just told me. Part of me wanted to burst out of her office and run home to my family and the other part of me knew I wasn't going to be allowed to leave. As I was battling all the emotions and thoughts in my own head the principal proceeded to speak, interrupting me. Apparently, the bad news was not finished; there was more.

It was then and there that she spoke the words no brother would ever consider; words that pierced holes and made sharp cuts through my heart. I could feel my heart sinking deep down to the pit of my stomach or maybe it was the blood that seeped through all the cuts and wounds of my now broken heart. Whatever it was I knew I could feel it in my stomach rather than in my chest.

She told me that my eldest sister, Zibo, was burned. The principal couldn't tell me much about my sister's condition, but she knew that it was serious. I was terrified. My most valuable asset was burned alive. My role model was burned alive. My mother figure was burned alive. The words "burned alive" have more powerful meaning than just written on a piece of paper. Those words came alive and I saw them written all over my angel of a sister's entire body.

The principal allowed me three days to go home because of such a tragic event. I ran out of the building after gathering my belongings and knew I wouldn't be able to go home to see my family until the next morning if I got lucky. I had no means of transportation and I was not in the right state of mind to devise a plan. I was walking down the street headed in the direction of my town which was miles and miles away. I waved at many trucks and cars to stop so I could catch a ride to make it there the next morning, but no one stopped.

It was at this time an angel from heaven sent me this man. He was a truck driver. The truck driver stopped, I told him the story, and I begged him with everything in me to help me get home. He was God's undercover gift. The driver drove me home and I arrived there the next morning. I couldn't even understand what was going on. My head was pounding from crying for endless hours on the ride home.

I hopped out the truck and without forgetting to give the driver my blessings for bringing me home I ran to my house. It was far worse than what my principal had described. The tears just would not stop and I placed my hands on my head. I took a deep breath, but I couldn't seem to catch my breath. If my house was way worse than what the principal had told me one can only imagine what my beautiful sister was suffering. I looked up, trying to talk to God and wondered if it was all just a dream. As I did so my neighbor caught my attention. He came over and explained to me what had happened. He told me that he helped put the fire out along with the other neighbors because the fire trucks couldn't make it through the narrow streets.

Unfortunately, for my house and my beloved sister, our street was one of the narrow ones. He informed me that my sister was severely burned in the fire and was sent to the city's hospital. I immediately began running toward the hospital. I knew I was running fast because I couldn't breathe, but I felt that my legs weren't moving fast enough. My mind was sprinting, but I felt that my body was walking, barely. I was under a trance where nothing was okay at all. My heart was racing as if I had been running a marathon. It is moments like these that are just indescribable.

When I arrived to the hospital I saw my mother and my brother crying into each other's arms. They explained to me what happened to my sister. That day she was trying to turn on the stove. As I mentioned before we heated the house with wood. Sometimes the wood wasn't dry enough and it was hard to start the fire.

That day she used some paper and sticks to start the fire, and then thicker woods on top. She poured some petroleum and lit it with a match and the fire didn't start.

Then, she added more petroleum and it started steaming. When she used the match for the second time, the ignition was so intense it was essentially a small explosion. Some of the ashes that were wet with petroleum were scattered around the area and the flames grew in height.

My sister tried to extinguish the flames and smother the embers around the stove, but embers dropped right next to the petroleum can. She didn't realize that the petroleum can was that close. The petroleum can blew up burning her severely and spreading the fire throughout the room.

My brother was outside and he heard the explosion, as well as my mother's scream. He ran inside and saw my mother in the corner of the room and pulled her out. Then, he went back and pulled my sister out, but she was already seriously burned. When my mother saw her body in flames she took a pail full of water and threw it on her. Her clothes had already stuck to her body and her plastic slippers had melted on her feet.

After they explained to me briefly what had happened I went into the room where my sister was. When I got there my sister couldn't move and couldn't open her eyes. She had third-degree burns that covered eighty percent of her body. When I saw my sister burned to that degree it was like I had lost the light of my life.

Burned alive. I could draw them out in my head as I sat in the seat in the principal's office. I could draw them out in my head as I sat in the truck as I made my way home, but I didn't have to anymore. I had them right in front of me. My sister's body laid so peacefully, as it seemed, in the hospital bed. However, I knew she wasn't peaceful. I had the words burned alive laying right in front of me, but what I wasn't expecting was the true meaning of them.

I stood there shaking with tears streaming down my face, balling my eyes out hysterically. I saw her flesh. I saw her tissue or at least whatever was left of it. I saw her bone. I saw her in a state that no brother should ever have to see his sister. I saw her slowly slipping from my fingertips and me being the man; the brother I wasn't able to do a single thing to keep her with us. I got worse and worse. I literally wasn't able to breathe.

It was devastating, especially for my family, all that we were going through. As soon as we were doing better, things became difficult in our lives. It's not just financial difficulties, but to lose my sister was a disaster for my family. Three days passed and there was no real hope for her survival, so all we could do was try to keep her company in her final days. They sent her to a special hospital in Tirana where my school was located. The very next day I took a bus to go back to the capital and resume school.

I went to see my sister every afternoon. The principal made an exception, because we were not allowed to leave the campus in the afternoon–only on the weekends. I had thirty minutes each day, which were visiting hours, and I took advantage of them from the second the thirty minutes began to the second they ended. I had a cousin who lived in the capital, but he didn't get the chance to see my sister because I spent those thirty minutes myself. Twenty days every afternoon I spent those thirty minutes next to my sister's bed crying together with her. Many times the nurse came into my sister's room because she was alarmed by the sounds coming from inside, and it was just me giving my soul to my sister.

I sat there trying to take all the life and soul out of my body and putting it into hers. I could see her flesh melted onto the sheets and every single time I saw it I felt my own body melt along with it. I could no longer tell whether I was alive or dead and quite frankly I truly wished in those moments that I was dead. My instinct was to pick her up, have her stand on her two feet, and hug her for eternity. I wanted to just wake up from this nightmare; walk to her straw mattress on the floor and lay next to her; kiss her cheek and know my mind was going crazy, but she was still there laying as beautifully as she always was.

My sister

Time seemed to be going by so slowly, but so quickly all at the same time. Her body began to melt away and the heat from her burns on her body melted her flesh deeper and deeper.

As the days went by her health was declining and it became harder and harder to see her in that condition. One day I walked into the hospital door for one last time unknowingly. I went to the nurses' desk and followed the same routine. Every nurse knew me by that time as I was there every single day, every single visiting hour. I never knew this day would come. That day the nurse didn't let me go to see my sister. She felt heartbroken for me to see my sister in a worse condition so she said to me they changed the rules; that as a precaution they don't let anybody in her room anymore. They used this as an excuse not to let me see her.

As the words came out of her mouth I could feel my hearing go deaf. The only thing I could hear was my tears falling to the ground and splashing against the floor and whatever pieces of my heart that were left simply drop to the same floor as my tears. I heard it break and I felt it even more powerful than hearing it. Goodbye... What brother would be able to live without saying goodbye to his sister?

I begged to be able to see her for one more second, just to say goodbye. I knew it was goodbye. The nurses refused to let me in as her body was way too deteriorated for me to see. Although they refused to let

me see her, I continued going there until her last day
hoping the nurses would change their mind.

Regardless, I wanted to say my goodbyes and
comfort her in the last moments of her life, but she was
alone. To this day my voice shakes and my heart aches
when I remember not being able to say goodbye. I had
no closure. I walked back to my campus and just felt like
dragging my entire body across the concrete roads. What
purpose did I have to live? My sister was burned alive
and was in great pain, and the most painful of all was not
being able to look at her and have her hear me tell her
soul goodbye. I was never allowed to say my last
goodbye to the woman who shaped me. My heart aches
every time I think of her.

A few long scary and extremely mournful days
later the news we were all expecting was released. Zibo
was dead. Zibo was sent to heaven. Days before I wished
to see her laying peacefully asleep right next to me and
to kiss her cheek and know it was all just a dream. That's
just what I got but not in the way I wished for it. She laid
asleep so peacefully and so beautifully forever now. Her
suffering was over. Although I wasn't able to kiss her
cheek and know she was right there beside me I knew
that she would sit right on my shoulder forever now and

continue to take good care of me all throughout my life. To this day as I write this I know she's sitting on my shoulder reading it. She's my angel and the love I have for her is like no other. She left me with a broken heart which never healed. I miss her more than words can express.

It was the morning after we received the news that really broke me. My cousin and I were to go in the same ambulance with my sister's deceased body. I wasn't even able to fathom the thought of an eight-hour ride back to Gjirokaster carrying my sister's lifeless, burned body. Just sitting next to her body without her soul in it for hours killed me. It was the soul that I was never allowed to say goodbye to.

Thoughts like these roamed through my mind for eight long, unbearable, emotional, and mournful hours. All I could do was cry hysterically. It was one of those cries that you don't even make a sound because the pain screams louder than the actual cries.

After the eight-hour ride home with Zibo's body we finally arrived. My eyes were full of tears, which I couldn't seem to wrap my head around. How could a single person have that many tears? I stepped out of the ambulance to find my entire family and neighbors waiting for my sister's body to arrive. I saw tears in their eyes and heads hanging low but I felt that I was far worse.

I had to go through an extremely difficult time of my life. I had just stepped out of the vehicle transporting my sister's deceased body only wishing her soul was still in there to say my farewells. After a few emotional, dark days of mourning the death of a beautiful woman whom we all called our own, her body was buried and in turn I knew this meant it was time for me to head back to campus and continue my studies. I wasn't sure that this was possible, but I knew that was the next step in this horrific and seemingly never-ending journey.

Before I left for school I grabbed my youngest sister, wrapped my arms around her body tightly, and hugged her for what seemed like an eternity. As I held my arms around her I felt as if it was all a dream and my arms were around my dead sister's body. It was my only way of saying goodbye without saying the words "goodbye". It was a mutual feeling between us because we both refused to let go of each other. It reached a point where we both kept crying and couldn't catch our own breaths while squeezing each other tighter by the second.

My family could not fully understand what we were feeling at that moment. At best they felt only a glimpse of the pain we were experiencing as they watched us hold each other endlessly. So, they tried to separate us. Finally, after many attempts they pulled us apart. We looked each other in the eye and just cried. I proceeded to say my goodbyes to the rest of my family before my departure to Tirana.

I went back to school, but I was never the same without my sister. For months I could not focus on my studies because all I could think of was her. She was my best friend and my greatest gift in life. On weekends, when everybody went out to enjoy their lives, I stayed on campus and felt like I had lost half of my body. I knew I had to find the strength to overcome the sorrow but no matter what I did I was unhappy.

DISSATISFACTION BUILDS

"I'm not afraid of storms, for I'm learning how to sail my ship."—Louisa May Alcott

It took time for me to get back on my feet, and I recovered enough to focus on my education. I was determined and I graduated with honors from the technical school. I had a 4.0 GPA, I had done well and I was satisfied with the knowledge that my scores would help me advance financially.

When we lost Zibo, my younger sister had just started the last year of high school, but she had to stop going to school and look for a job. My cousin (Rashide) helped her find a job in the shoe factory, which was the same factory I was expecting to work in after I finished school. Her income was very low because she didn't have any credentials. She met someone at work and two months before I finished school she was married. After graduating, I returned home and began looking for a job.

One night my brother and I went to my cousin's house (the one who was a Secretary of the Party Committee) and asked if she could help me find a job. It was clear that she didn't want to help me, and not because she couldn't. She didn't give me any hope, and I didn't ask twice or beg her. However, my brother begged her and indirectly told her how I felt about the political system in Albania. He said, "you either help him, or he would go by his uncle", which was code for escaping the country and going to Greece.

After that, I found a job in construction. A company from the capital was going to build a bridge in my town. Initially, I worked alone for only three days a week loading and unloading heavy materials from the truck. I moved sand, grout, rocks, and all kind of construction materials. After a while, they hired another employee. The two of us loaded and unloaded about 10 trucks a day using nothing but our bare hands and shovels.

There was no supplier from which we could purchase the materials, so we took sand, grout, and more from the river. Whenever I tried to take a break for a few minutes my fingers were almost too stiff to move, and it always took longer than it should have for me to loosen my grip and push aside the shovel. When I tried to open my hands, my bones made a cracking noise. It was very hard, intense labor. It seemed as though every muscle in my body hurt, and I was always drained after work-especially because this was not the work of which I had studied so long.

Once a week a trailer came with 260 bags of cement, each weighing 50 kg. My friend and I had to unload the trailer and transport the cement to the warehouse, which was about hundred feet away. He stayed on the top of the trailer and brought the bags to the edge; and I carried two bags of cement on my back on each trip to the warehouse until we were done. My body was constantly covered with cement, which I had to wash off in the river-even during the winter.

While working for this construction company I went to school part-time, three times a week. I wanted to continue my education and practice the skills that I had. During this time, four of my friends from school and I went into the town's agencies almost every week to complain. We needed answers: why didn't they give us the jobs we had studied for? After a year of complaining, they gave me a job in the shoe factory. The position that they gave me in the factory was physically difficult, but I was young, strong, and healthy. I had no problem with it. I didn't have the top pay, but I had decent pay. I was paid every other week on a piecework basis, which motivated me to produce a higher output. Sometimes when the factory was short in supplies, they laid off everyone for a month or two until they received more. Knowing this, I worked harder and longer hours when the materials were available.

Financially, this was a good time for my family as both of my siblings were married. Only my mother and I were living at home, and I had the opportunity to save some money and start paying back our loans. It took me two years to pay off our debt. After that, I started saving money for the family.

Shortly after I began to work at the factory, I realized that there was no appreciation and that they were incredibly unfair to the employees. The communists that were in power increased the quantity of shoes we were required to make per hour without informing us. At the end of the two-week pay period our paychecks went down because we didn't reach the new requirements. They attempted to cheat us in the payroll. There were 15 employees in my section. The work in the factory is like an assembly line, which means that if one section is not working, the whole operation shuts down.

Once, I was extremely upset because I had worked hard all day and was tired of being exploited, so I decided to turn off the electricity. Everyone was scared

and wondered what would happen to me. I told my co-
workers what I did and why, and everyone agreed that it
was unfair of the administration to increase the
minimum production without notifying us. My sister and
I worked in the same factory, but in different sections.
When she heard what I did, she came over and pulled me
aside. She said that I was insane and warned me that I
would end up in prison if I acted out, especially because
our father was an anti-communist. I told her not to
worry, but she insisted that everyone knew that I was the
one who did it.

Shortly after, the supervisors asked who turned
off the power and why. Nobody mentioned my name, but
everyone started complaining how unfair it was for them
not to inform the employees about the increase. The
supervisors didn't take any of it into consideration.
Basically, they told us there was nothing we could do
about it, they had the rights to do so, and we had to go
back to work.

The communist system treated citizens
unethically, and not only in the workplace. They wanted
to control every aspect of our lives. Like every other
young adult, I wanted to dress nice and neat. My hair
was maybe an inch long in the back and I had a small

mustache. In Albania, we weren't allowed to have long hair, a mustache, a beard, or anything like that. One day I was working and a group of 10 people approached me. It was the manager of the factory, the engineer, the director, one gentleman from the government's office, and some other individuals. The gentleman from the government's office was in charge of producing communist propaganda for the factory. His words were very powerful and carried much weight, even though he was often wrong. No one was able to disagree with him, because they knew they would be in trouble.

They wanted to speak with me and ask why I had long hair and a mustache. The gentleman from the government was very angry that I had long hair and threatened to send me to Spac. I heard of Spac. It was a place buried in the mountains of northern Albania. Spac was in ruins and had a collapsing copper mine where political prisoners were used as a slave labor. They were forced to work to the point of exhaustion under brutal conditions. It was extremely hard, dangerous work, and sometimes fatal. Failure to comply would lead to prison isolation, violence, torture (cutting off water and food supplies for days, placing freshly boiled eggs under prisoner's armpits, or electric shocks through their body), and sometimes even execution.They threatened to send me there if I didn't follow their orders.

One of the engineers in the factory was my neighbor. He was very friendly and an admirable man. After everyone left, he took me aside. He said to me, "I want to talk to you as a neighbor, as a brother, or as a friend-however you prefer. You are a great person and I don't want anything to happen to you. You know how these people are; you know how the government is. Be careful, be smart. They would incarcerate anyone for even minor infractions."

It was kind of him to advise me. It's very likely that he saved me from being sent away. I promised to cut my hair and mustache and nothing happened to me, just as he said. The communists didn't behave in this manner only with anti-communist families. They conducted this behavior with everyone. I remember one Albanian agent from my town. When he saw individuals on the street dressed nicely, and maybe their clothes were a little tight, he stopped them. He claimed that they were following other countries' styles, which was unacceptable to the communists. Western, capitalist countries like France, Germany, the UK, and the USA were all labeled as "bad countries". To embarrass these individuals and make them dress "properly" in the future, he would rip their clothes in the middle of the street, where everyone could see them.

One time, this agent was assigned to go to Greece. His duty was to bring back someone from a village nearby who had escaped Albania. When the agent found the escapee, he subdued him, and brought him back to Albania. After that, they set a date and time to hang him in the middle of a village called Vrisera. They hung him in front of the public, then tied him to the back of a truck and dragged his lifeless body around all the streets of that village. They wanted to terrorize and scare the rest of the community and send a message that a similar fate awaited anyone who tried to escape. Even if you crossed, they wanted you to know that they would find you.

A lot of people wanted to escape Albania. Three individuals from Vlora (a town southwest of Albania) planned to escape through my town and someone leaked the information to the soldiers on the border, so they had highly tight security that night. That very day, an 18-year old without any connection to the individuals from Vlora attempted to escape; of course, he was completely unaware of the increased security. He was caught during

the crossing. According to stories, they were going to
kill him, but when the soldier pointed the gun, the
machine gun got stuck. The young man had a knife with
him for protection and threatened the soldier. Then the
soldier said to the teenager, "If I want to kill you, I can
kill you at any time. Go ahead. I will let you go, don't
worry."

The young man didn't want to hurt anybody, he
just wanted to make it out alive. He believed what the
soldier said to him and began to walk. The soldier shot
30 bullets into him. They brought his lifeless body to the
village and tied it to the back of a tractor. The tractor
dragged him throughout the surrounding towns and
villages to send a strong message to the public of what
they would do to anyone who tried to escape.

Attempting to escape Albania was a big risk, not
only for that individual, but also for their entire family.
The immediate family members were sent to jail, and
some others not jailed were displaced. The communists
confiscated everything the families owned, including
their houses, and relocated them in the mountains far
away from their homes. These families weren't allowed
to have a radio, TV, or anything. All their friends and
even their cousins, had to cease their relationships with

them. If they continued speaking with these families, they would also be ostracized. When it was time for young adults to start their families, they had to make sure they got involved with someone in a similar situation.

They couldn't marry someone from the communist class. This happened rarely, but if someone from a communist family did marry someone with links to anti-communists, the former would be disowned from their family. The victim's families weren't allowed to go anywhere without permission from the authorities. When they did, they were treated without respect from other passersby.

These families were the first candidates to go to prison, generally for the smallest of infractions. In Albania, prisoners were used for working in mines. Eyes and ears were everywhere with deadly effect. The secret police continually violated the privacy of individuals, homes and any form of communications, making arbitrary arrests to fill the prisons with the necessary numbers of workers. The accused had to go to court before being imprisoned, but that did nothing to help them. Albanians didn't have the right to have an attorney represent them, so the communists did what they wanted. Everything was formal and legitimate, as long as they said, "We sent them to court and they were convicted."

The crime rate in Albania was extremely low. The majority of prisoners had been imprisoned for political reasons, and the time to serve for the crime was a lot shorter than the time for political reasons. The chances of ending up in prison were very high. It's difficult to fathom now, but people could be sent to prison for nothing more than a few words. Citizens informed on other citizens and even family members could not be trusted, in this darkest of the Communist Nation. It is said that a gentleman went downtown for a coffee; on the way back he met his neighbor. His neighbor asked where he had been, and he answered downtown for coffee.

His neighbor proceeded, "I thought you went to buy some meat." The poor gentleman was only joking when he answered, "I went for meat and I found only the butcher." His neighbor went straight to the police station and reported that the gentleman complained that there was no meat in the store. This individual was arrested right away; before he even returned to his house. They sent him to prison for about twelve years.

Many Albanians had similar experiences. My sister-in-law has three uncles. One of them was in the United States before the WWII. He couldn't return home when Albania became a communist country. As a result, he couldn't come back to see his family. He wrote letters to his family, but they didn't always receive them because secret services had to open all mail received from outside the country. If they thought the letter was suspicious, they ripped it. Sometimes they read it and gave it to the families to test them and see if they would return the letter to the secret services. If they didn't report the letters, these families were in trouble.

One of the other two uncles was on his way to work one morning and, as many places didn't have public transportation, he was riding a donkey to work. Someone from his neighborhood mocked him for riding the donkey, and he responded, "My brother in America drives a car; I have a donkey, and this is what I ride." The next morning he was arrested and had to serve eight years for that.

Frequently, Albanian citizens served endless years in prison for the simplest reasons. If someone had something to say against the government and its communist system, they were imprisoned for the rest of their life. The few who weren't sentenced to life in prison returned with serious health issues stemming from abuse and hard labor they endured. They weren't allowed to return to their hometowns prior to their imprisonment. Instead, they had to live and work somewhere else worse as added punishment. A large number of prisoners didn't make it out alive. When they died, they were buried in locations known only to their executioners. The families were notified of their deaths, but they were given no further details and could not ask where the bodies had been buried. If they did, they would be the next ones to go to prison.

Even events which were meant to be lighthearted carried the danger of imprisonment, or worse. Every December, Albania held a festival where the best singer was selected among a range of participants. The 11th Annual festival was held in December 1972 and it was criticized from the First Secretary of the Party of Labour of Albania, Enver Hoxha, who was the only leader that Albania had from 1944 until his death in 1985 (a 41-year reign).

Enver Hoxha became agitated, realizing that liberalization had increased to this level that he described as destructive. He did not limit his brutal attack against the 11th festival. Many intellectuals such as the editor in chief, ideological secretary of the Party Committee of Tirana, a member of Center of Committee of the Party, writers and dramatist were imprisoned. The hosts were dismissed from their job, singers were banned from practicing their profession, and illustrator and architect were replaced.

The festival participants had introduced a different style of dress, art, music, and literature that were contradictory to the establishment.

These art styles were seen as threats to the leadership because they introduced modern viewpoints that could be seen as transformation. Responsible for these was also the Ministry of Education and Culture, which had miscalculated the risk of liberalism. Albanians felt uncomfortable everywhere they went and could never predict what would happen next. We were always fearful.

Life in the village was hard. Working in the farms without any equipment or technology made it harder for the citizens. Many young job applicants were offered jobs on farms when they didn't receive the jobs for which they had applied. They were told that working on a farm for two or three years would help them obtain the jobs they had applied for. So, they were forced to accept the jobs, despite not wanting to do so. Sometimes the jobs were far away and they had to walk to and from the jobs. Much of the time the money they made per day was not worth the commute, but most did not have another option. Albanians weren't allowed to relocate from their hometowns. No one could relocate from the village to live in the city, or from one city to another city.

Residents of villages all around Albania were not a priority for the government. The public services were underfunded and understaffed. In my town, there was only one small clinic with one doctor for emergencies. The clinic in the city was bigger, but very busy. They had to cover a large area, which included the surrounding villages. Whenever there was an emergency individuals had to wait an extended period of time for the ambulance to arrive.

Once, my neighbor, who lived on the second floor, had to wait almost five hours for the ambulance to arrive. She was pregnant with her seventh child and started to have contractions in the early stages of her pregnancy. She delivered the baby at home with the assistance of another neighbor. Everyone was worried because the baby was born premature and both the mother and the baby needed medical attention.

All of these substandard living conditions and restrictions began to get the best of me. By the time I was 17 thoughts of escaping from Albania begun to surface. My first cousin lived in Kardhiq and was assigned to serve in the army in my hometown, Gjirokaster. Whenever he had a few hours break he came to visit us. My brother and I spoke with him about life outside Albania. We had to speak very softly to ensure that our conversation could not be heard by others, especially the neighbor who lived on the second floor. He was a retired cop.

Even within our group, it was a bit scary to discuss those conversations because anyone could pretend to be trustworthy and actually be your enemy. My cousin had an aunt who lived in Turkey since the WWII. Eventually, we came to the point of casually discussing what it would be like if we lived there with her. We all thought that the aunt in Turkey would help us and began talking about it, but it was never an actual plan because my cousin was hesitant. Once we realized how fearful he was, my brother and I never discussed the subject again.

A few years passed and at 21 I could not stop thinking about fleeing the country. Escaping Albania was a huge decision. To make that decision, I had to think about many details: my future, potential consequences, and whether or not the attempt was worth the risk. Life in Albania was miserable. I knew that there was no freedom and no opportunity of the future I wanted to experience. I didn't want to start a family there. I didn't want my children to suffer the way I did. Often, I asked myself: should I escape? Should I leave my family? What would happen to them? Would they be punished because of my escape?

I spent much time thinking about my safety and the odds of actually making it out. In order to escape, I needed to know the area very well. Most people who tried to escape were captured and killed. Others thought they crossed the border when they were actually still in Albania, since there were unmarked parts of the border which made it difficult to know if you were in Albania or in Greece. Some villages are located on the border of Albania and Greece and the residents of those villages speak Greek. This made people who were attempting to flee confused. Hearing people speaking in Greek made them think they were on Greek soil and emboldened them to stop and ask for help. Instead of being helped, they were reported to the secret services.

Planning the escape required a tremendous amount of work and the highest level of secrecy. Getting to know the escape route was very difficult, since Albanians weren't allowed to go to villages located less than five to ten miles from the border. To travel near the border, citizens had to have very compelling reasons, as well as permission from the police or secret services. To make matters worse, villages near the border were packed with voluntary spies, who gave signals to the army and made capturing potential escapees easy work. If someone looked even a bit out of place, he or she would be questioned, reported, and often arrested. Permission slips were mandatory.

I had plans to escape, but at that time I didn't make any major moves. I had to be fully prepared. Everything that I did up to that point in my life— exercising early in the morning, swimming often, lifting extra weight at work - was part of the plan. I did all this to physically prepare for the escape. My first hope was for my brother and me to escape through the area in which he was stationed while he served in the army. That hope didn't last long - he could never be serious about it.

With three young children, it was almost impossible for him to make that decision.

I didn't know any other area through which I could escape on foot. There were high fences running along Albania's borders. Only a small percentage of the borders didn't have fence due to the tough terrain. The only option I had at that point was to escape through the sea from Saranda (a town southwest of my city). It was the closest point to Corfu in Greece - provided that I could swim four to five miles through the sea.

Everywhere I went, I paid a careful attention to everything surrounding me. Anything I could learn was valuable information. In the evening, I went out for walks or coffee with my friends. We spoke about the day, and sometimes about the events occurring in our country. When talking, I had to be careful not to cross the line - I just couldn't trust them. They were great friends, but I noticed that none of them had plans of escaping. It was difficult to find a friend with the same mindset - someone I could talk openly with about escape.

Once, I met someone through a mutual friend, and the three of us got to talking. This gentleman told us that he had served the in the army on the border of

Yugoslavia. Then he started telling us army stories. My interest piqued, I started to ask questions - being extra cautious, of course, because I didn't want him to get the impression that I was trying to escape.

I asked him about the fence. "How do you know when someone is trying to escape?" "What if that someone is a fast runner?" He told me that the fences (called "klon" in Albania) are incredibly high and placed around five miles before the actual border. There were two sets of fences with barbed wire approximately a half-inch away from each other, and two wires like an "X" placed in between.

On areas where the land was flat, about four or five yards in front and behind these fences, the ground was very soft. As a result, it was easy for them to follow the footprints of escapees. Behind the fence, there was extra barbed wire placed on the ground. When the wires touch each other the army immediately receives a signal, and the soldiers inspect the exact location where it has been touched.

The army was based behind the fence, and they had very well-trained dogs. When they received the signal, troops and dogs rushed toward the location. They could be on high alert for days or weeks, depending on the information they had. No one could outrun the dogs - they really did have a plan for everything. That day, I asked the former soldier if they had captured anyone during the time he was serving. "We did many times. Only once did someone succeed."

He tried to explain to us how this escapee had crossed the border. This information was invaluable to me, so I listened very carefully. He said that this individual carried wires during his escape. When he was by the fence, he tied his own wire in two different spots of the fence. When he cut the fence in the middle, his own wire allowed the electricity to continue through the rest of the fence.

In June of 1983, I finished school. To obtain the diploma, we had to take a math, reading and writing exam, and a physics assessment right before the end of the year. We took the exams in the cafeteria. Present were the minister of education, the principal, and the professors. The minister had a sealed envelope which was opened at the beginning of the exam.

We had four parts on that exam, and while he was reading and giving instructions, I was solving the problems. By the time he had finished reading all four sections, I was already done with the first two. Shortly after he finished explaining, I was done with my exam. As soon as I stood up to give them my exam paper, the minister of education told me to sit down and finish. I informed him I was done. He ordered me to sit down and check my work. One of my professors smiled, but didn't say anything. I sat down for about five minutes before standing again to hand in the exam. He wasn't happy, but he took my exam. Even though I knew I did very well, I knew nothing would change for me. Right after the exam, I went swimming. I needed to prepare for something much more important.

MANDATORY SERVICE

"Great acts are made up of small deeds."—Lao Tzu

After finishing school, I was supposed to serve in the army. Sometime in September of that year, I received a letter from the authorities. Normally, guys went into the army at the end of December or beginning of January. In the meantime, I had to prepare myself for service. I had to shave my head, go for check-ups, and complete other necessary milestones.

The military received the rest of the information (who I was, which family I was coming from, my education) from the police station. Then, based on this information they would determine where I was going to serve in the country. At that time, my brother asked my cousin (Rashide) to have me stationed near home, to ease my suffering. Surprisingly, she did. They assigned me to Saranda, a town very close to mine. I had to go through training for about four months, and afterwards I was assigned to protect a building. As it turns out, this building was the one in which they determined where individuals in the military would serve.

Normally, on the day men leave for the army they packed all the new recruits on the back of military trucks and drove them to their destinations. However, when my day came they canceled the truck. Myself and two others left the next day. That morning, they sent us to the building where we were assigned to go after training. Then from there they sent us to the borders of Ksamil, the training site. After we showered, they gave us our army uniforms. They didn't have my size, so for a while I had to wear a uniform that was much too large for me. The Albanian army didn't use socks. Instead, they gave us a set of two white cloths to wrap around our feet.

We had to learn the proper way to do this, which wasn't easy. Often, our feet would hurt and blister. They also gave us a set of white cloths for the collars of our jackets. We had to use one set for the day, and wash the other set every evening. That same day, we received and signed for the rifles, helmets, and all the other equipments. We had to keep our weapons with us at all times. Even when we were sleeping we had to keep them next to our beds. Many times second-year soldiers would steal bullets or the white cloths from the new soldiers.

During the first few days, we spent all our time in the classroom, learning the standard guidelines and the requirements of the army. After that, we started the regular schedule. Outside of the base was a bell, which was used for communication with the soldiers. Different rings corresponded to different signals. For example, one ring meant mealtime; two rings meant to drop everything and get in line; three rings meant emergency; and so on. Every morning at five o'clock, we had to get up, put on pants and line up outside.

We had to do it within a minute of the time the bell rang and the line had to be perfectly straight. If the line wasn't perfect, we had to start over. After that, we had to run for 2-3 miles; go back to the base; wash our faces; and fix our beds. If the corners of the bed didn't look like the corners of a box, the older soldiers had to undo all the beds in the room and make us do it again. Everything had to be done within time, and perfectly. If one soldier didn't do it right, everyone had to start over.

Next, we had to dress up in the army uniform: pants, shirt, belt, hat, coat (in the winter), and shoes. All the clothes had to be clean and the shoes polished. The buttons had to be in a straight line, the belt had to be the perfect height on the waist, and the hat had to be straight. Afterwards, we had thirty minutes to clean. They divided us in two groups: one had to clean outside, and the other one inside. Many times after we had finished mopping the floor, the older soldiers took pails with water and spilled them on the floor.

"Do it again," they would taunt. When the bell went off, it was time for breakfast. Before breakfast, we had to line up and march. With each leg straight and unbent, we had to stomp on the ground in unison. The officer had to hear only one thud. We had to repeat until he yelled, "Time to go inside!" Breakfast was only fifteen minutes.

Normally, breakfast entailed a scoop of bean soup, tea, and feta cheese with a slice of bread. Often, they would tell us, "If you want more, just ask." That was a cover- up. That was just the politicians saying, "We give enough food to our soldiers." Nothing could be further from the truth: we were always hungry.

Soldiers weren't allowed to leave the base unless it was a family emergency, or if they were sick and needed to seek medical attention. Sometimes, older soldiers, with the permission of the captain, had to go and purchase necessary supplies for all the soldiers. We gave them a paper with our name and a list of supplies we needed. Once a week, we had to go and cut wood for the kitchen. The place where we gathered the wood was twenty minutes away from the base, and the terrain was rocky. All the soldiers were spread apart which made it easier for someone to disappear for a while.

On those days, we would pick the fastest runner and send him (illegally) into the village to buy cookies for all of us. This went on until we were caught. The new soldiers were always ecstatic to see the cookies, since they were constantly starving. I really didn't have much of a problem, since I had never had enough food throughout my life. However, some soldiers had a really difficult time adjusting to constant hunger.

After breakfast, we had to clean up and exercise. Different days corresponded to different exercises, but most of it had to do with running. Every day we had extensive exercise for six to eight hours, regardless of weather conditions. Sometimes, we trained under an older soldier who'd been designated the group leader, and sometimes directly under the officers.

We took showers twice a week and the dry cleaning service came once a month for our uniforms. We had to take showers outside all year 'round. The room had three walls and no ceiling. It was essentially a big barrel with a faucet. The water came down with very low pressure, and I can't remember a time it was actually warm. We changed underclothes only. If we got our uniforms dirty in the evening we had to wash and wear them again the next morning. Many times we had to wear damp uniforms because we didn't have heat or anything to dry them.

One day, an older soldier serving as "captain" punished a disobedient younger soldier with push-ups. Just as he was finishing the set, the captain placed his foot on the soldier's shoulders. The soldier couldn't continue because of the weight, but the captain yelled at him to finish. Then, he placed his foot on the soldier's head and pressed his face into the mud. Everyone was disgusted - especially me. Enraged, I pushed the captain. I yelled at him for unfairly beating on one of his men.

Turning to me, the captain said, "I will kill you. I will beat you up so badly, you don't even know. You will see what will happen to you." Every thirty minutes after that, he would come up to me, curse at me, and repeat the same threat. He was gigantic comparing to me, but I wasn't scared of him. I knew I was right and I had the support of the other soldiers.

The next day, one of the officers trained us. Every two hours, we took a ten minute break. During one of the breaks, everyone was relaxing having a cigarette. The officer pointed out a place in the field, where there was a rope about 13 meters long. He said that after three months of training, all of us had to be able to climb to the top of the rope. The older solder that was our captain the previous day happened to be in our group. When the officer told us about the rope, I took the opportunity to show the soldier who threatened to kill me who I really was.

I asked the officer if I would get a reward for climbing it now. Laughing, he said that he didn't think any of us could do it; "It's much harder than it looks," he scoffed. Incredibly, he said he would give me the day off to go into town and enjoy myself if I succeeded. However, if I failed, I would be punished. He didn't have any faith in me, and I couldn't blame him: I was short and swimming in an oversized uniform.

My army unit while in basic training. That's me (Vladimir) in the top row, 3rd from the left.

I started climbing the rope with relative ease, but was winded and exhausted by the time I was close to the top. However, hearing my comrades cheer for me and remembering the officer's threat of punishment gave me a burst of energy.

I got to the top. It was extremely cold day and while descending the rope tore the skin off my fingers, causing my hands to bleed. One of the soldiers ripped a piece from the white cloth of his uniform and wrapped my hands with it. We had basic first-aid on the base, but not with us.

The officer kept his promise and let me go for a day. I was happy to have the day off, but much happier that I had proved a point to the "captain" who had threatened me. The older soldiers took advantage of the new soldiers because we were new, quiet, and didn't want trouble. So naturally, they abused us.

In the army we learned how to identify the airplanes of England, France, the United States, and Russia. We learned about their size, weight, and speed, as well as the kinds of warships from which they were launched. We learned about the infantry of enemy nations, and the kinds of weapons they carried.

We had to learn this to be prepared to protect our country. They also taught us that Great Britain and the United States were our most aggressive enemies, always offending our nation and committing atrocities. They used all kinds of propaganda to brainwash the soldiers.

We were there to protect the sea, so we also had to learn about artillery. We had to learn all the detailed information and the measurements of the artillery. I still remember them: each shell was 36 kg, four feet long, and 100 mm in diameter. At first, we used an 80/85 mm artillery, but eventually switched to the 100 mm. We learned how to load and unload it 26 times per minute.

The artillery had two firing positions: inside and outside the tunnels, which were on a large hill. The artillery had four tires, and we went on our knees to push it back and forth with our shoulders. When the trucks came with the shells, all the soldiers had to help unload. The shells came in packs of two. We had to bring those inside the depots and take the old ones outside. Needless to say, it was hard work.

The officers from the division had to be present to sign for the new artillery cannons. Those days, we were on high alert. One day, after a few hours of exchanging cannons, my foot started to hurt. I felt the cloth on my foot getting crumpled, and I could sense that my heel was wet. At that time, I told one of the officers that I needed to briefly stop and fix the cloth. However, he and the other officers didn't believe me. Visibly angered, they ordered me to keep working.

Though in pain, I went to pick up the next case of shells. However, when I returned to the loading truck, I threw it in instead of placing it gently. One of the officers started screaming at me, "You fool, you are going to blow up the whole town! If one shell blows up, they all blow up!" I calmly repeated that my foot hurt, and he ordered me to take my shoe off. When he saw that my foot was bleeding, he berated me for not placing the cloth on properly.

I tried to explain that it had shifted after hours of work, but he wouldn't listen. He pointed me to a rock where I could sit; I couldn't work anymore that day. The next day, I asked the officer if I could wear one shoe and one slipper. He refused at first, stating that I had to be in a full uniform. However, after he saw that I couldn't walk, he relented. I worked wearing a slipper on my injured foot that day, but even that didn't help much.

I noticed that my foot was getting infected, so I informed my officer. Normally, the word would have to travel slowly up the chain of command until it reached the chief, who was the only one who could officially sign a soldier out to see a doctor. I complained for two days, but nothing happened. On the third day, I went straight to the chief's office myself. Initially, he was furious that I had broken the chain of command by coming to him directly with a complaint.

However, after showing him my foot, he gave me permission right away to see a doctor. That day, I went to the army hospital; the doctor prescribed antibiotics and injections twice a day. We didn't have a nurse on the base, so I had to go to the closest village approximately 40 minutes away. After I explained my situation to the doctor he kept me there for a week, because it wasn't worth it for me to travel back and forth during my treatment period. When I returned to the base I immediately went back to my routine. I had to use the slipper for another month, but that didn't get in the way of my training.

After we had finished switching out the artillery cannons, we went right back to learning fighting skills and tactics. One beautiful day, an older soldier assigned as captain, gave us a two-hour training break in place of the customary 10 minute one. The next day, he was yelled at by an officer and punished. Naturally, he was furious with our group. He told us that he would punish us during training until he found out who betrayed his trust.

We felt terrible for what happened to him, and determined to find the rat in our group. We selected one of our comrades to hide behind the officers' building to find out who from our group ratted on the older soldier. After a few days of doing this, he determined that no one went into the officers' building except the soldier who was assigned to clean it every morning. That is how we discovered the culprit. That evening, the older soldier treated all of us cruelly for hours on end. Multiple times he ordered us to put on and take off our uniforms. To get into bed and to get out of bed. After a while, he let all of us go to bed-except the one who had betrayed him.

The older soldier placed a chair on the top of a table and told the culprit to get up on the chair and stand on one foot. He gave him the right to change his leg every thirty minutes. He then gave him a book of army rules to read for the rest of the night. Afterwards, he asked him questions relating to the book, beating him if he answered any questions wrong. The next morning, I heard that he had tortured the rat for about six hours before letting him sleep.

In the end, the soldier broke and admitted his betrayal. To avoid trouble for himself, the older soldier determined that he would punish all of the first-year soldiers in place of the rat—a classic tactic to turn us on him. That was when our real punishment started.

Obviously, all of us were upset by this turn of events. I was the oldest in the group, and the rat came to talk with me in private. He told me that the officer had forced him to report everything to him. However, he said that he felt guilty for what he had done, and feared for his life. He was stuck between a rock and a hard place:

the rock being his fellow soldiers (who were threatening to kill him), and the hard place being our officer (who was secretly forcing him to report the details of each day).

The rat knew that in order to avoid trouble with his fellow soldiers, he had to stop reporting to the officers' building for cleaning duty. Together, we devised a plan: he would continue with his cleaning duty, but instead of giving accurate reports, he would lie and give glowing reports about our group to the officer. Eventually, we would rotate the soldier on cleaning duty.

In the meantime, he went around apologizing to the other soldiers, promising to correct his mistake. I went around to the other soldiers in my group as well, asking them to give the rat a second chance. Eventually, the other soldiers agreed with the plan, and the rat stopped receiving death threats from our group. He said he owed me his life.

Our time at the base was quickly coming to an end. The officers from the division came to see if we all passed the final training tests. After we had proved ourselves, we took the oath in front of the Albanian flag and, one by one, kissed it. Afterwards, two of my friends and I were sent to serve in the city of Saranda, where we had stopped by four months ago. In a very short time, we got to know the officers, soldiers, and everyone else who worked in the offices. The chief had only been there for a month, but everyone seemed to like him very much. We learned that the former chief was a corrupt man, doing favors for families that would give him money and specialty foods. Anyways... starting the day we arrived there, we were scheduled to protect the building and rotate every three hours. Between the three of us, I was on duty for three hours had a break for six hours.

As a result of my excellent training record, I was quickly promoted to be captain of the guard group - all five of us. Three soldiers protected the building, one soldier was assigned as the chief's private driver, and I was in charge of the soldiers and tasked with taking care of the officers' mail. I delivered messages between them, as well as correspondences to their respective families.

I was very glad to take on this extra duty. It kept me busy since the work of a soldier wasn't always exciting. I had the chance to go out into the city, to explore and meet new people.

*Here I am taking some much needed time off to
enjoy the scenes around town in Saranda.*

I began to garner respect from the officers;
however, I never looked down on the men under me. I
knew what was like to be mistreated by those in power,
or by those who were slightly older. Under the rules, my
men were supposed to stand still in one spot - not

moving an inch. I was as lenient with my men as possible, letting them move around and even go out into the city (with the officers' permission). I knew that they never had enough sleep, since their schedule called for them to switch out every few hours. Many times, I would take one of their places so they could get some sleep or just relax.

When I had to deliver something in the city, I sometimes had the chance to go to the beach for a while. One especially beautiful weekend I was able to relax on the beach, surrounded by the city folk. However, a dark cloud hung precipitously over our happiness: soldiers frequently paraded the bruised, swollen bodies of those who were caught trying to escape the horrors of our communist regime.

It was a grim sight, their visibly tortured and bullet-ridden bodies. That day, I saw a couple of bulletproof military boats, which protected the sea from Saranda, Albania to Corfu, Greece. They had just caught and executed three citizens who tried to escape by swimming to Greece. After executing them, they hung their bodies on the front of the boats and went around the beach so everyone, including children, could see them. They were battered and bloody all over.

The same thing happened a few months afterwards when they caught another individual trying to swim to freedom. I was on the beach and saw everything. That day, a young teenager was sitting next to me. Visibly angry over what was happening, he started to talk to me about it. However, when he noticed my uniform, he began to hesitate. After I assured him that I was alright with him speaking his mind, he started to open up to me.

Like many in our nation, he was very unhappy with the current system. I didn't know if he had plans to escape, but for his own safety I warned him to watch what he said to others. I told him what he already knew - that there were a lot of dangerous and untrustworthy individuals out there. I reminded him to not trust anyone, even friends. He thanked me for the advice.

The constant parading of dead bodies on the beach was all the proof I needed that escaping by sea was rarely, if ever, successful. Fifteen years had passed since the last successful escape from my city, Gjirokaster. This incident was primarily remembered through the terrible burdens imposed on the escapee's family. After a few visits to the beach, I decided to take my chances over the mountains. My escape would push me to the brink of both human will and survival. I would climb in darkness over jagged, loose rocks, scale steep cliffs, suffer ineffable agonies - all in the search of freedom. I knew that freedom - even though I could only imagine it - was worth my life.

ONE STEP CLOSER

"The journey of a thousand miles begins with one step."—Lao Tzu

After serving for three months in my new post the chief gave me permission to visit my family for three days. I was ecstatic to see them. When I visited home, I was delighted to see that my brother had purchased a TV with the money I saved before joining the army. I don't know how he managed to find it since there were never enough TVs, and there were waiting lists to purchase them.

While I was home, we built an antenna. For the first time in my life I was able to watch TV at home. With that antenna we were able to watch the Greek channel, too. One of those days my brother pulled me aside to talk in private. He said he would introduce me to one of his friends and that we would have a serious conversation.

He told me that I would have to be totally honest and trustworthy at all times. We met his friend the next evening. His name was Mike. My brother explained that they had a plan to escape. "Would you like to come with us?" he asked. At first, I didn't know how to respond. I didn't know if they were serious, or if this was some kind of government trap. I told my brother, "If this is a trap, then report me and send me to prison. If you're serious, then let's get the hell out of here."

That night was my first time meeting the other guy, and I felt a little uncomfortable. My brother assured me that Mike was reliable and I had to trust him. "I'm sure he feels uncomfortable too. He is one and we are two. We have to trust each other."

We started discussing the escape. Mike knew the way because he was a former soldier who had served in a village close to the borders. I knew how to cut the wires on the fence close to the border. There was a lot to discuss before the escape, so we had a long conversation that night. I noticed that Mike was skeptic - he kept reminding me to not discuss this conversation with anyone else. I didn't blame him for feeling that way; in fact, I was thinking of a way to somehow test him. My brother had a family; I couldn't have him being reported for subversion. I promised Mike we would stay in touch.

After three days had passed I went back to my post. I couldn't wait to go back and further discuss the escape. One day, my brother and Mike surprised me by visiting me at my post. I asked the officer for permission to go into the city with them, and he approved it.

We went out for four or five hours. Walking through the city, both of them started asking me if I was ready to escape that night. They mentioned to me that was the reason they came. I asked them if they were insane; we didn't have a plan or anything. It would be certain death. Laughing, they told me they were just joking.

Later, we stopped at a restaurant and had dinner. The restaurant was located right across from Corfu. We wanted to talk about the escape, but we couldn't risk it since we didn't know who could be listening. Both of them kept looking to the island of Corfu, making underhanded signals. I warned them to be careful. After dinner, they headed home and I returned to my post.

We agreed to meet again as soon as I returned home. A few months later, I got the chance to return home for the second time. During those three days we had the conversation again, making sure to keep our plans hidden from my sister-in-law and my nephews.

At the time Albania was the poorest and harshest of the totalitarian communist nations. Even as the Russian and Chinese governments began to ease their use of murder and terror, the government of Albania used its isolation from the world to employ these tactics in their most brutal and repressive form, with a goal to keep its citizens in line.

In July of 1971, US President Nixon agreed to visit China and meet with Zhou Enlai. Our leader Enver Hoxha felt betrayed, and our relations with China began to deteriorate. After many political obstacles, in 1978 China announced that it was cutting off all aid to Albania.

During this time, Albania didn't have any trading partners and was the most isolated country in Europe. After China ended its relationship with Albania, the economy of the country started to decay and governmental issues begun to rise. The top thirteen leaders of Albania started fighting among themselves. In 1981, Hoxha ordered the execution of several leaders and they notified the Albanian citizens that foreign agents had executed them.

In 1948, Hoxha developed diabetes, and in 1973 he suffered a myocardial infarction from which he never fully recovered. During the late '70s, he turned most state functions over to Ramiz Alia. In 1983, he suffered a cerebral ischemia and in 1984 he was stricken again, while spending his final days in a wheelchair. On April 9, 1985, he was struck by a severe ventricular fibrillation. Two days later (April 11, 1985) he died. All this information was revealed some time after his death.

It was considered classified material for Albanian citizens. In 1985, during my second year of service, I received a phone call from my brother. He heard from Mike that Enver Hoxha was very sick. I am not sure how our friend discovered this information, but it was the truth: Hoxha passed away a few days later. (Between my brother and me, Hoxha's codename was Beluli.) A day after Hoxha's death, my brother called me to inform me about it.

"Beluli is dead." I didn't doubt his word, but even so, the truth was difficult to accept. Usually, the army would be the first to know about an event like this. After hanging up, I waited to hear the news from the officers - and for them to place us on high alert. The next day early in the morning I heard patriotic music on the radio, which was unusual. Now, I was sure something important had occurred - likely, the death of someone politically significant.

However, when I asked one of the officers why this music was playing, he told me he had no idea.

Twenty minutes later, however, the same officer approached me after speaking with the chief. He instructed me to get everyone on high alert-something tragic had occurred. Right away, I woke all the soldiers up and informed them that we were on high alert.

A few minutes later, the chief walked up to me head down, red in the face and very serious. He ordered me to gather all the soldiers and officers in the room within thirty minutes. He had an announcement to make - only for the army, at that moment. They had to make sure the army was on high alert before the citizens heard the news on TV.

After running around to notify everyone, I was the last one to enter the room. By that time, the chief had already made the announcement. Everyone was crying, and I knew what was going on - but I had to pretend I didn't. After displaying clueless signs and asking around, I had to pretend to be devastated and weep because I truly disliked Hoxha and the system that he represented.

Enver Hoxha was a brutal dictator, but Albanians were brainwashed. Many legitimately wept for him. Many believed in, respected, and loved him. He was a great public speaker, and they enjoyed listening to him. That day, I had to be an actor. At the moment I "heard the news," I put my head down, pretended I was crying, and walked out of the room. I went into the bathroom, rubbed my eyes for a while to redden them, and laid down for a few minutes. The time was set for the TV and radio station to announce the news to rest of the country. All the citizens of Albania had to stop everything they were doing to listen to the national news.

All schoolchildren and workers were dismissed early that day. The chief gave another speech, informing us how critical the situation was for the nation - and how we were the ones to protect it. Now that our leader had passed away, the "enemies of our country" would be ready to strike without mercy. Since the United States had bases around Albania (Italy, Corfu), we had to be on high alert. He also advised us to be ready for a potential attack from Yugoslavia.

I strongly disliked the system, but I did love my country. I was ready to die for it, if need be. After Hoxha's death, Alia took his place. He tried to follow in his footsteps, but the changes had already begun. Citizens had no idea what was happening. Life was confusing; no one really had any idea what the next day would bring. Each day conditions steadily declined. The economy showed no signs of improvement.

Ramiz Alia tried to improve it by introducing price reforms in a few sectors and loosening some political controls. These changes led to marginal improvements, but I understood that the current system wasn't going to last. I didn't have much information about what happened next. During my last months in the army, I was able to see my family a few more times.

Here I am sitting on an army motorcycle in Saranda.

Toward the end of my time in the army, I began to become irritated of being used by the officers. They used us for everything. Due to my position, I had more freedom than the other soldiers, which meant that I was especially targeted by the officers. One of the officers suffered from asthma. Frequently, I tried to help him and he took advantage of my kindness. He sent me to fulfill many of his duties, as well as on personal errands. Often he sent me to purchase merchandise for his family and ordered me to take care of them when they needed help. It was getting out of control.

One time he called me, but I didn't report to his office right away. I took my time and he was unhappy, but didn't say anything to me. Instead, he expressed his anger to one of the soldiers, saying that he would punish me by transferring me to a base near the Greek-Albanian borders. He assumed that sending me to the mountains would make the remainder of my time in the army unbearable, but I was thrilled. When the soldier informed me of officer's decision, I thought to myself, "This is exactly what I've been waiting for-an opportunity to learn an escape route."

I pretended to be angry with the officer and began not to comply with his orders. Whenever he called me for his errands I gave excuses, which made him even more irate. Sure enough, after a short time he transferred me to Grazhdan, a place very close to our border with Greece. I was transferred there a month and a half before the scheduled end of my time in the army.

All soldiers have the right to take two weeks off during their two years of military service. I had used all of my days off with visits to my family. Before my transfer, I asked one of the officers with whom I had a great relationship for a favor. I asked him to tell my new station that I hadn't used my days. He agreed. The chief in the new place was from one of the villages of Gjirokaster.

After a week, I asked the chief if I could use my days. He was skeptical and asked me how it was possible that I hadn't used any of my leave, especially because I was so close to the end of my service. I excused myself by saying that we were busy and didn't have enough soldiers to replace me on those days. He had to confirm with my previous station and, thankfully, the officer there kept his promise.

I went back home for about ten days and had a wonderful time. While at home, I spoke with my brother and Mike about my new station and the opportunity to gain more information for our planned escape. I told them to come and visit me, as it would be a great reason for them to obtain permission from the police to be close to the borders. I assured them that I could take my weapon with which to protect ourselves if needed.

They seemed very wary. I noticed that they didn't trust me because I was the youngest of the three. Their reaction wasn't positive, but my hopes were still high. My time back home passed very quickly and, soon enough, it was time for me to return to the army. This time I was happy to return because I was hoping that my brother and Mike would visit me.

I had everything carefully planned. I waited a few days before calling them. I couldn't talk much over the phone because I was afraid someone was eavesdropping. Unfortunately, they never came. I could not overcome the sense of failure I felt after losing my chance. I knew they were afraid, but it was worth the risk if we could leave the country.

During my time in Grazhdan, I studied the terrain very closely. There was a mountain close to us with a rough terrain. There were so many rocks and cliffs to steer clear of that. The top of the mountain was the border of Albania and Greece. I spent most of the day looking at the mountain and thinking about how to climb to the top, which paths I should follow to avoid the cliffs. After a certain point, simply looking at the mountain made me visualize my escape route.

Almost at the top of the mountain was a white strip. I asked the soldiers about it, but none of them knew why it was there. Below the white strip was a pathway used for the soldiers who were closer to the border. They used this pathway to get around their base and down to the village, ten minutes away from us. I asked questions here and there, though I was always careful to be discreet. I hadn't been there long enough to know the soldiers very well or feel comfortable asking them specific questions.

One of the soldiers who had been in Grazhdan for his entire length of service told me that sometimes the soldiers at our station went up there to play soccer with the soldiers closer to the border. As soon as I heard that I recognized an opportunity to go see the fence and everything around the border.

I expressed to the soldier that I was eager to go and play soccer with them and kept pushing him to call them and set a date for us to meet. Luckily, when he called they agreed to play, but we had to play during a certain time of the day, because to get to the soccer field we had to go through a barbed-wire gate. They were only allowed to open the gate during specific time frames. The day they decided to play was my lucky day.

The barbed-wire fences were about four meters high, very thick, and very intimidating. On both sides of the door behind the fence, I saw wires buried in the ground. It would be impossible to cross those wires, even with daylight. The border was about ten miles away from where we were playing. I was very alert and kept note of all the details of the surrounding area, even as soldiers constantly circled the mountain to protect it.

One of the officers worked with a police dog (K-9 unit). After we finished playing soccer, the officer put on a little show for us to demonstrate how they trained the dog and what they could do. The officer ordered one of his soldiers to leave a footprint where we were standing. Then, the soldier was ordered to walk around the mountain. When the soldier returned he went straight into the building and locked the door. Next, the officer guided the K-9 unit near the soldier's footprint and let it loose.

We watched every move the K-9 unit made. The officer said that the dog was young and had a great sense of smell. He also said that if someone zigzagged in an attempt to throw the dog off their trail, the K-9 unit would go straight and would not be confused because he was able to detect their scent from approximately 250 meters radius. Sure enough, the dog followed a straight path and quickly found the building in which the soldier was hiding. The K-9 unit jumped outside the door and the windows of the building, becoming increasingly agitated as he looked for his target.

The officer placed the K-9 unit on the leash and told the soldier to come out. When the soldier came out, he had protective clothes on and was holding a thick mat in front of him. Even with the leash, the K-9 unit was in a frenzy; biting the mat and pulling at the officer in charge of him with full force. After a while, the officer locked the dog back in his cage and went inside.

One of the soldiers said that the dogs were trained with a soccer ball and disliked soccer balls because of this. Even the sight of a ball from far away made them bark angrily. That day I learned something new about those dogs. The soldier wanted to show us how the K-9 unit reacted toward the ball. He took the soccer ball and placed it between the bars of the dog's cage. The dog lunged towards the ball. Then, he put his nose between the bars, grabbed the ball, stuck his teeth in the ball, and popped it. Even though jamming his nose between the bars of the cage had injured his nose and he was bleeding, the dog kept ripping the ball while barking furiously.

The officer heard the dog barking and came outside to find out what was going on. He wanted to make sure everything was okay because he didn't like the way the dog was barking. Then, he saw how bloody the dog's nose was and we were punished. After a while, my team returned to our base. That day was a learning experience for me, which placed me a step closer to accomplishing my goal. I went back to my routine and started counting the last days.

In Grazhdan, we had one officer who took great personal pleasure in getting soldiers into trouble for the smallest of reasons. He was the one who gave lectures full of propaganda to the soldiers. We called him the Commissar. The Commissar did everything within his power to send second-year soldiers in prison. Every thirty minutes he went outside to check if the soldiers were at their assigned posts. He checked in the corners; behind the windows; and every single move they made. Sometimes, the soldiers went inside for a minute to get something or moved to the other corner of their assigned post to avoid the wind or the cold. Other times, they paced back and forth at their post so they would not fall asleep.

One night, the Commissar caught one of the second year soldiers, who had gone inside for a minute, and yelled at him. He ordered him to go inside, give up his duty, and hand in his weapon. He replaced him with someone else and wrote up the soldier without warning. They had a book where records of all the soldiers and everything that happened on the base were kept. It was where the Commissar reported this incident. The next morning, this was reported to the officer.

The officer was furious when he saw this insignificant incident logged in the book. We could hear them arguing from our posts outside of the office: "Why did you write him up? Now that this is in the book, there is nothing I can do. Don't you know that we have to report this to the division? If someone shows up and reads this without it having been reported, both of us would be in trouble! I don't want to send this soldier in prison on his last week in the army, but you've left me with no choice."

The officer was the one who had to report incidents to the division. During the argument, the Commissar told the officer, "If you don't want to report it to the division, I will." After a while, one of the soldiers had to go into the office for something. The soldier saw the Commissar with a black eye. The officer told him the story and admitted that he punched the Commissar for what he did the night before. The officer was against the idea of sending soldiers in prison for no particular reason.

The soldiers were extremely angry with the Commissar. They wanted to bring him behind the hills, where no one could see and beat him up. The Commissar realized how angry they were and did not leave his office for the entirety of the last three days of their service. Not even for food or drink. The officer, in order to avoid an escalation of the situation, brought him drinks, but no food. He was still disturbed from the Commissar's actions.

At the end of December 1985, I was released from the army. On the last day, everyone was happy and celebrating. We were going insane and felt like we had been released from prison. Everyone was shaking hands, hugging, and saying their goodbyes. Many of us were crying. It was an emotional moment because we had spent a long time together and some of us had formed strong bond. Soldiers in the army come from all over Albania, which meant that there was no guarantee that we would ever see each other again. The Commissar was the only one who stayed inside and didn't say goodbye to anyone, because he feared for his life.

After we said our goodbyes, we were driven home in a military truck. All the soldiers were in the back of the truck cheering and celebrating the end of our service. They took us for a ride all around town, beeping the horns as they dropped off each person at his respective home. When I reached my destination, my entire family, including uncles, aunts, and cousins, were waiting for my arrival.

Everyone was excited and had happy tears in their eyes. I was released close to New Year's Eve, so we had twice as much reason to celebrate. We all enjoyed that night. A few days after I was released, I could go back to work. A couple of months passed and I didn't report back to work. I was hoping to set a day for my escape instead.

TEMPORARY DISAPPOINTMENT

"Failure is simply the opportunity to begin again, only this time more intelligently."—Henry Ford

During this time, my brother, Mike, and I had many discussions about escaping. Late at night, I listened to the news on the radio which were the Voice of Russia and the Voice of America, translated into Albanian. I listened to learn what was happening outside our country. What I heard on the news was completely different from what our government was describing us. At that point, I had a clear view of what was accurate and what was not.

I learned that Greece and other countries had camps for refugees. This was exciting news for me: knowing I would have a place to stay after my escape made me feel more comfortable. However, talking and discussing the plan didn't bring us anywhere. Mike promised us that he knew the safest way to cross the border. I noticed that each time he came over to talk he had a different attitude. He started asking strange questions and continuously displayed signs of distrust towards us. Perhaps, he thought that my brother and I were going to betray him, trap him, and report him.

His inability to trust us was frustrating me. I was trying my best not to disclose my anger towards him because I didn't want to jeopardize our friendship, but it was difficult. When you are an honest person and others keep testing you, it hurts. He continued not to trust us, and one day he said we had to be brothers by blood.

It was an old superstition in Albania that when you tasted each other's blood by licking it, you become siblings by blood. Two people had to prick their pinky fingers and taste each other's blood. I didn't feel comfortable with his idea. I refused and told them that we had to trust each other without superstitions, but as we are.

I knew from his actions that he was very weak. His discomfort and apprehension made me concerned that he would go and report us to the police. I kept pushing for them to decide on a date and finalize the details of our escape, because I didn't want to wait any longer. The longer we waited, the more likely we were to be caught. I felt like there was a bomb ticking and ready to explode. We never knew who was listening. They weren't giving me much hope, and I was becoming increasingly agitated; so I decided to go back to work. I couldn't wait around any longer without a job. In 1986, I started working again at the shoe factory.

One day that year, my brother and I received an invitation from one of my friends from the army. He invited us to his sister's engagement party. They lived in one of the villages close to the borders, so we needed to get permission from the secret services in order to attend the party. Trying to obtain permission was a great test for me. Sometimes, when you received permission once and proved to them that you could be trusted, it was easier to secure the approval for subsequent requests.

They would check the records and would not hesitate to approve you in the future. My brother and I were among those with a 50/50 chance. We had a chance to be approved because our cousin was a Local leader, but we could also be denied permission because our father was anti-communist. We applied for permission and were lucky to get it.

We went to the engagement party and had a great time. It was nice to have an opportunity to meet different people and talk with members of their family. I had met my fellow soldier's father for the first time when we were in the army and it was a pleasure to see and talk with him again. He was a shepherd. That night he told a story about something that occurred when he was close to the borders. The shepherds were allowed to go around the mountain because of their sheep, but in the meantime they were spies, too.

The shepherd said that he had always wanted to do that. One of the nights when he was around the mountain with his sheep, he heard the soldiers shouting as someone was trying to escape. The shepherd knew something was wrong, therefore he hid behind a tree for protection. The shepherd carried a long staff with a big ball at the end. While hiding behind the tree, he saw the individual trying to escape pass by him.

He became frightened and hit the escapee in the head with the end of his staff. The escapee went unconscious and the shepherd tied his legs. After that, the shepherd started yelling for help from the soldiers. He kept screaming that he caught someone who was attempting to escape. When the soldiers arrived, the escapee was conscious and the soldiers started to beat him up. They hit him in the face with the back of their weapons. They tortured him and then took him away.

My friend's father didn't know what happened next until six months later, when he was called to report to court as a witness. When he went to court he saw the escapee clearly for the first time. He was in his early thirties; very big and tall. The escapee said to him, "If I knew you were that small, I would have carried you on my shoulders and brought you to Greece with me. Now, it is too late. I am arrested, and you are out there, but I will never forget your face. One day, I will come and get you."

We talked all night, and the next morning my brother and I headed home. I went back to work. My brother and Mike worked in construction at the time. One rainy day, they came home early and, out of nowhere, they asked, "How about we go today?" Of course, I agreed and told them that I was ready. Something about the way they approached me felt off, but I was eager to leave.

I told them that the best way to escape would be from Grazhdan—the area where I served during my last months in the army. The mountains there had too many rocks and cliffs for the army to place any fence. If we took that route, we would not have to worry about cutting any fences. At that point, I knew how to cut the fences, but the process was still dangerous. I told them that we should choose the difficult terrain, because the smallest mistake with the fence would lead us to our demise. However, I was the youngest and they never listened to me. That afternoon, we wore strong shoes for walking through the fields and the mountain; took some wires to connect to the fence; and grabbed a tool with which to cut the fence. Mike told us that the border where we were going to escape was on the other side of the mountain. We couldn't see the border, so my brother and I had to trust Mike.

First, we had to walk through the town and the fields beyond for three hours. Then, we got close to the area where permission was needed to enter as it was close to the border. It was getting dark already and we had to go around the village. We used umbrellas up to a certain point, then we threw the umbrellas into the bushes. We didn't want to leave anything visible behind and we definitely didn't want anyone to see us. While walking around that village I had a strange feeling that we weren't going to make it to the other side of the border that night.

In those days, escaping Albania meant that you would never see your family again. A lot of thoughts started going through my mind. I thought about my mother and my nephews, and how I didn't get to kiss them goodbye, because I didn't want them to ask any questions. Instead, I was kissing them within my heart. I wondered if it was enough.

I looked at my brother walking ahead of me and thought that maybe this wasn't the best option for him and his family. He was leaving his wife and three young children behind. After his escape, life would be very difficult for his family. I realized that I didn't want my brother to escape that night. I wanted him to return home and think it over.

Then, I thought that if I escaped alone, the system would punish my brother and all of my relatives. I was having mixed feelings about escaping. Every time we stopped for a break my brother and Mike talked about their wives and children. That made me think that, even then, they weren't completely certain about what we were doing either. I knew they were going to change their minds at some point during the escape.

Before we started to climb the mountain, we had to cross a wide canal filled with water. It was at the corner of the field and used to irrigate the crops in that area. We removed our clothes and kept them bundled in our hands while we crossed to the other side of the canal. When we were on the other side of the canal, Mike went insane searching for something. We asked him what he was looking for, but he wasn't responding. I told him that we couldn't afford to waste any time and that whatever he lost wasn't important enough to prevent us from moving forward.

He said he couldn't continue without finding it. He was looking all over, tapping against the ground and trying to find it with his feet. We kept asking him what he lost and why it was so important to him. He was very reluctant to answer us, but after a while he realized that he needed our help to find it and told us that it was a gun.

All of us went back into the water to search for the gun until managed to find it. As I feverishly searched and poked my hand around the dark, murky waters, all I could think about was the terrible outcome that could have been. I wondered what would happen if he found the gun first, but kept it a secret. How could we possibly trust him now that there's a hidden weapon in our midst?

We continued walking and asked why he hadn't told us about the gun. He insisted that it was not a problem, "It is just a gun. I didn't have to tell you. It is just for protection. This is something that I carry all the time and everywhere I go."

Then he began telling us about how good the gun was. I was frightened. I thought that if the soldiers caught us, Mike would kill us and insist that he had never intended to escape in order to protect himself. Mike was the one who should have been leading us because he knew the way, but I noticed that he was always in the back. I didn't know why, maybe it was his earlier distrust of us, but something made me think that he didn't feel safe and feared that we would do something to him.

If he had planned anything for us, it was too late for my brother and me to avoid it. Whatever was meant to happen could not be stopped. We were too close to the border for plausible deniability. I wasn't certain that he had planned a trap for my brother and me, but I was feeling very uncomfortable. I tried to tell him that he had to stay in the front and lead us, but he refused.

After climbing the mountain for about three hours, we came to a dead-end. We turned around and tried four different routes without making any progress. We were wasting time. I realized that he didn't know which way to go. He kept saying, "Don't worry about it, I know the way; I have been through this way many times before." We were going in circles, wasting time, and not progressing. I knew that we weren't going to make it to the other side in time. By the time we get to the border with Greece, if we ever did, it would be daylight and we would surely be caught. My brother asked him again if he knew the way.

He swore he knew the way, but I had felt anxious about the escape all night. First, he had a gun and didn't want to tell us. Then, he refused to lead the way, trailing behind us instead. He didn't know the way and I was sure of it. I also felt that he was going to pull the trigger on us if anything went awry.

I really believed that if one more thing went wrong it would lead us to death. My mother had lost one child already and I didn't want her to lose two more. With all this racing through my mind I decided to start displaying signs that I didn't want to proceed with our plans that night. As soon as I mentioned returning, both of them agreed. They were so eager to turn back that it didn't take us long to come to a decision.

We returned home around four in the morning and my sister-in-law heard us. She got up and noticed that our shoes and clothes were dirty. She asked where we had been, but we couldn't say that we had been partying since we didn't even smell like alcohol; so we tried to give valid excuses. My sister-in-law didn't know what exactly had happened that night, but I knew she was suspicious. I wasn't sure if my brother had said something to her in the days before our escape attempt, but it was clear that she understood something strange was going on with us.

We cleaned up and went to bed. Our long trek the night before left us exhausted. My muscles were sore and I felt discomfort when walking for a couple of days. The thoughts that went through my mind and the stress I had endured made me even more tired. In order for an escape to go smoothly, the trust between those involved has to be unwavering. You should worry only about the soldiers; not about each other. Unfortunately, that wasn't the case with us.

Later, I had a discussion with my brother and we agreed not to make another attempt with Mike. It was too much of a risk. A few days after our failed attempt we saw Mike again. This time our conversation didn't feel the same as before. He was talking and acting very strangely and he seemed unlike his usual self. Some time later Mike and my brother had a big argument at work, and from there our friendship diminished.

The more time passed, the more certain I
became that I would never be happy in Albania. I
couldn't take it anymore. I was missing my chance to
experience freedom, happiness, and a better future. By
this time I was certain that I wasn't going to be able to
build a healthy, happy family in Albania. I kept asking
my brother to escape with me, but he no longer seemed
open to the idea. I think the night we attempted the
escape made him realize that he was making a mistake. I
couldn't blame him for that, especially since he had a
wife and children to think about. Personally, I could not
abide by staying.

I began searching for a friend with similar plans
as me. I had a friend at work who repeatedly told me
about the Greek movies he watched late at night. Our
friendship was getting stronger. Hearing him talk over
and over about movies and stories from outside our
country made me think that maybe he was like me.
Maybe he wanted to escape, too. But he was from a
communist family, and his father was pro-communist, so
I never had the courage to ask.

My mind was set. If I couldn't find a friend to
come along, I was going to escape alone. There were
times when I thought that escaping alone would be

better. It could be safer for several reasons. For one, it would be more difficult for the soldiers to discover me if I was alone. I also wouldn't have to worry about someone betraying me. I continued to prepare myself for the biggest decision of my life. I went swimming every afternoon; and ran from home to work and back again. Every day I tried to run faster and tried to break my record from the day before.

I wasn't going out with my friends anymore. I tried to stay away from them as much as I could. I was staying home and refraining from socializing for many reasons. I was exercising a lot at home, and I didn't want my friends to have any potential ties to my escape. After my escape the police would go after all of my friends and family, asking questions, and probably accusing them of possessing prior knowledge of my plans, even though they wouldn't have known anything about it. In Albania, anyone surrounding you would be in trouble if you fled the country.

My friends asked my brother about me on many occasions. They began to think that I was upset with them because they hadn't seen me in a while; they kept asking my brother why I wasn't hanging out with them anymore. In reality, I wasn't upset with them at all; I was just trying to protect them. I had to think about the consequences of my escape and do my best to prevent my loved ones from being punished. I didn't want anyone to be hurt because of my actions.

During that time two sisters from Jorgucat (the village where my sister-in-law was originally from, very close to the border with Greece) escaped. Rumors went around that the women had been in relationships with the soldiers and that the soldiers helped them. I don't know the truth of it, but I was intrigued by this story and the aftermath of their escape. Their escape made me feel more comfortable about escaping because of how differently the government responded. The government didn't relocate their family as punishment, which was unheard of. Citizens started showing signs of unhappiness, and I began to note small differences in the government's actions following the death of Enver Hoxha.

These changes gave me hope that my brother would be safe. If this pattern of behavior continued, the government might not relocate him or send him in prison after my escape. My sister was married to a communist. I was also worried that my brother-in-law would divorce her, but maybe he wouldn't now that the government was less damning of those associated with escapees. I knew they couldn't do anything to my mother because she was disabled. I knew for sure that my cousin (Rashide) was going to lose her job. Even though I didn't worry much about whether she would lose her job, I still had to think about it. I had to consider every consequence for those I was going to leave behind.

Missing my family was going to be another challenge for me. Thinking about never being able to see them for the rest of my life made planning my escape very difficult. When I thought about my mother and everything she had suffered, it was incredibly painful for me to consider leaving her. On the other hand, thoughts of my future and my feelings about the system left me with no hesitation. I knew that I had to leave.

My biggest challenge would be crossing the various borders and making it out alive on the other side. To ensure my success (and safety) I performed many calculations as I was planning this attempt because I was fully aware that I could lose my life. My odds of success were grim: It seemed as though I had a 99% chance of death and a 1% chance that I would make it through alive.

Though I was determined to carry out my plans I was still searching for a companion. I started spending more and more time with Mihal, one of my co-workers. He was Greek/Albanian, fluent in Greek, and originally from a village close to the borders with Greece. He also had an aunt who lived in Greece for many years. Learning about these developments made me even more interested in asking him to join me on my quest for freedom.

As I considered having a companion on my trek I soon became convinced that having Mihal as my traveling companion would make things be far easier for me to adjust and become self-sufficient than it would be if I went alone.

Every day, I tried to take my break at the same time as Mihal to get to know him to better ascertain how much I could trust him. Mihal seemed to be a very nice person; one who would always have your back regardless of circumstances. Yet, it was difficult for me to speak openly about my plans.

One day I took a chance and said, "From what I see on TV, your aunt in Greece is living a good life. Greece seems to be a great country." He turned around and replied, "It's a shame...the quality of life we have here; the way we live."

His response gave me the courage to continue our conversation along this path, although I still had to exercise extreme caution in what and how I spoke. One day I suggested that he give me his aunt's phone number so I could look her up in case I were planning on going to Greece. Although I was serious I was careful to make sure my comment came across as though I was joking.

Right away he said to me, "You're not going to do it alone. Let's escape together. Are you man enough to do that? I would love to escape, but I never expected something like that from you. You are very quiet and have only shown signs that you are very happy with this country."

I told him that I was only joking and he became extremely upset with me and said not to make those types of jokes with him anymore. He continued saying that he was serious and that he didn't like it when people tried to test him. After he said that, I felt that I could trust him even more, thus we became closer. I told him the truth, that I wanted to escape and that I was looking for someone who wanted to do the same; someone who spoke Greek; and had someone we could trust on the other side.

He was exactly the type of person I had been seeking. I told him that if he was ready to escape I would come with him. He kept saying how shocked he was to learn I had such thoughts in my mind. I was not surprised to hear this, because I had no choice but to act as if I had never entertained a single dissident thought.

That day Mihal mentioned to me that he was serious, but not one hundred percent certain he wanted to escape. He was married and had a two-year old daughter whom he couldn't leave behind. He explained that he wanted to escape with me, but he didn't know the way. I was very excited to hear that he was interested and immediately told him that I knew of a way.

At that moment he declared that I was going to make a huge difference in his life. I could help him cross the border, and he could help me while we were in Greece. He guaranteed this and told me that he would make me rich in Greece, because his aunt was wealthy. I thought that was an interesting statement to make. Just because his aunt was wealthy doesn't mean that she was going to enrich me.

To ensure that money never became a point of contention I simply told him that I didn't need help with money. I just needed some help with the language until I stabilized my life.

Mihal and I spoke every day at dinner time. We met at a private location with enough environmental noise that no one in the surrounding area could overhear our conversation. We would hang out after work from time to time. On several occasions we went to his house to meet his family. His family was very nice, and I had already known his father while he worked at the factory before retiring.

The first time Mihal visited my house it was clear that my brother disliked him. My brother told me not to trust Mihal and asked me not to do anything reckless. I insisted that I didn't have plans to do anything —reckless or not. I behaved as though I was upset that he would even suggest such things because I wanted him to believe what I was saying. I wanted to make sure that my own brother did not pick up on a single clue as to my real plans.

To be honest, I also had mixed feelings about Mihal. I thought it was interesting that the first impression that my brother could gather of Mihal was one of utter distrust. There were days when I thought he was serious and there were days he wasn't sure if he wanted to escape Albania (and leave his daughter). As the days and weeks wore on I started feeling less certain about him.

Sure enough, one day he told me that he wouldn't be able to continue with our plan to escape; that he could not leave his daughter; and that he didn't have the courage to do it. As I listened to his well contrived reasons (or excuses), I felt at peace that he had made my life much easier by backing out. At least I didn't have to ask him to quit because I had already felt that he was not the ideal person to take such a huge risk with.

He wished me luck and asked if I would say goodbye before I left. I apologized to him and told him that I couldn't. I liked Mihal, but the less I spoke with people about anything even remotely related to my plans, the better chance I had to make it alive.

Mihal wanted to give me his aunt's phone number for a couple of reasons. In addition to doing whatever he could to help me, he also wanted me to talk with his uncle, who spoke Albanian, and ask him to apply for tourist visa for Mihal and his daughter. His secret plan was to take his daughter to Greece to visit and never return to Albania. I told him that it would be my pleasure.

One day, he gave me a piece of paper with his aunt's phone number. I didn't want to carry the paper with me, so I read it a few times until I memorized the number. I didn't want any evidence with me. Although it was unlikely that someone would find the slip of paper, I refused to take any risks. If the wrong person discovered the number I would not be the only one in danger. I didn't want the secret services to track the number and link it to Mihal.

After I had memorized the number I explained to Mihal that from that day onward I had to keep my distance as much as possible. It was not because he didn't want to escape with me, but I simply wanted to make sure he and his family remained safe after my escape.

I assured him that he would continue to be my friend and that I didn't want him to be in trouble. After that day we were still friends, but I kept my distance. It was the second time that I failed to find an escape companion. Whether this was some kind of divine intervention or some other warning sign, I decided not to try finding an escape companion. It was simply too risky because this type of search would inevitably entail telling more people, and the more people knew the more likely I was to fail. The last thing I wanted was to endanger myself or others close to me and wind up in prison (or worse) before I could escape.

It wasn't easy, but I decided that I was going to have to make it over the mountains alone. Therefore, I needed to be in the best physical shape of my life. There was no room for compromise, either. I determined to become stronger, fitter, and faster than any of the hundreds of terror police and soldiers who would be deployed along the border areas. And, since I would also have to evade dogs that were trained specifically to capture escapees, I knew a tough, disciplined, completely secret, daily training regimen was an absolute necessity.

Every day I exercised more vigorously than the day before to increase my endurance. Every time I pushed myself beyond my own limits I had to remind myself why the pain was necessary. As I recalled my mother, brother, nephews, and other close friends whom I was preparing to leave behind I found inner strength to keep going.

No, it was not easy. In fact, preparing for the biggest test of my life took more than brute strength. It meant really digging deep within myself; deeper than I've ever gone before to find the strength, courage, and fortitude to achieve something that was no longer a matter of choice. Escaping from Albania was my only option. I determined to beat the odds and ensure that my one and only chance would not end with my death.

Every day, my exercises became more taxing. And when I wasn't exercising I was thinking about how to adjust and improve my exercise routine. I was exercising, thinking, and working. This was how I spent every day of my life for that period of time. As I continued to prepare myself physically I had to consider every single detail of the escape from beginning to end.

The first aspect I thought about was when would be the most appropriate date and time to initiate my escape. Not only I would need to use the cover of darkness, but I would need the worst weather possible to mask my actions and presence in the mountains. That meant rain; lots of rain and heavy fog.

Since footsteps could be heard even in the most remote regions I also had to study the regional weather patterns. I soon discovered that the optimal time for my escape attempt would be November. November was known for delivering the necessary wet weather without the snow that could cover the mountain tops and potentially making my escape virtually impossible.

In the fall of 1987, I started keeping a very close eye on weather reports from Albanian and Greek radio stations. It was absolutely critical that I left before the first snow. If there were snow on the mountains my plans would fall apart rapidly and catastrophically. Now, it was only a matter of waiting for the perfect time. To help pass the time I began teaching myself to say a few key words in Greek to aid in my transition.

Again, I had to carry out my language lessons in complete secret, being careful not to make even the slightest mistake that could lead to my discovery, imprisonment, or worse—my death. In a short period of time I learned nearly fifty Greek words. It's possible that I would have learned a lot more if I could receive help from someone who was fluent in Albanian and Greek, but I couldn't ask too much about the language because people were going to ask why I wanted to learn. I couldn't afford to rouse anyone's suspicions.

Fortunately, I didn't have to ask too many people out there to teach me Greek, because my sister-in-law was Greek. That meant that my brother and my nephews also knew how to speak the language. My brother learned from his wife, and my nephews learned from their grandparents when they stayed there for about two years.

Therefore, it was easy for me to pick up some Greek words, but I was careful not to make it too obvious and not push it too far. This was hard; really hard. Can you imagine how I felt learning a foreign language from my in-laws without being able to appear too interested? My family meant the world to me, yet for all my trying to become integrated into their Greek culture I had to hold back so I could protect us all.

Swimming on a daily basis became an important part of my preparation routine. Regardless of weather conditions I made sure that I got into the water and pushed my body constantly. This was a huge mistake.

In July of 1987, I became ill with pneumonia. It was the scariest time of my life. My bout with pneumonia was even scarier than the possibility of being shot by a border patrol agent; falling headfirst from the top of a mountain; or even being locked up in prison.

Contracting pneumonia could really derail my plans because everything was resting on my health.

I had to take care of myself right away. I went to see a doctor and immediately took a couple of weeks off from work. The doctor was our neighbor and lived three houses down from us. He explained that I had to be serious about taking care of myself as he prescribed antibiotics for a week. I had no other choice but to follow his advice.

After finishing the antibiotics I wanted to know what more I could do to improve my health and rid my body of pneumonia. I learned about an elderly man who was known to be an expert in herbal treatments. I asked him what he suggested I should take to treat my pneumonia. He explained that the best remedy was honey from the first flowers of spring—the best honey produced. According to him, the fresh source of nectar and pollen provides all the vitamins and minerals our bodies require for optimal health.

He instructed me to take two teaspoons of this honey as soon as I woke up every morning, and he recommended me not to eat or drink for a few hours afterwards. I asked him if I could go to the beach and stay in the sun. He told me it would be fine, but advised me to protect myself from sunburn and to avoid the water as much as I could.

On the first day, I had to go into the water only a couple of times for a few minutes each time. With every successive day I had to increase the time I spent in the water, although I was always careful not to overexpose myself to the sun's harmful rays. He convinced me that if I followed his instructions, my lungs would be clear in no time.

I had some days off from work saved, so I took two weeks vacation. I bought the honey and went to Saranda, where I had been stationed for most of my military service. During the first few nights, I stayed at the base and enjoyed spending time with some old friends. The rest of the nights I stayed at a hotel. I followed all the instructions I had been given by the older man, and soon I started feeling much better.

10 days into my vacation the physician I had gone to see about my pneumonia checked into the same hotel with his family. I couldn't believe it. I thought to myself, what are the chances that that particular doctor would choose the same hotel that I was staying in, at the same time? I just could believe how much of a coincidence it all seemed. His room was directly across

the hall from my room. Yes! We were on the same floor, too.

Albanian hotels were designed so that multiple rooms could share a single bathroom. When I left the bathroom to return to my room, I noticed the doctor's room was open, and he saw me.

At first, he almost didn't recognize me because I was so tan. He was in shock—not only because of how tan I looked—but, also because he could not believe that someone with pneumonia was now at the beach. He retrieved his stethoscope and came into my room, asking to examine me again. I allowed him to check my lungs and he couldn't believe how clear they sounded. He asked me what I did, and I told him. He could hardly believe that the old man's advice had actually worked, but it was impossible to deny that I had made remarkable progress.

I felt a lot better, and even more so when the doctor confirmed my good health. I stayed for a few more days before I went back to Gjirokaster. When I arrived home I resumed my exercise routine while keeping a close eye on the weather. It was now Fall. It was time to initiate my escape. Now, it was only a matter of waiting for the right moment, with each passing day bringing me closer.

During these final days in Albania my body was working hard, but my mind was working even harder. By this time I had developed a highly detailed plan of action for before, during, and after my escape. This included rehearsing just the right words to say to my family; how to get close to the area by the borders; and how to handle the possible setbacks I may encounter along the path from my town all the way through Greece. I had to do it all without the smallest mistake.

Even after passing into Greece, I had to have a plan. Sometimes the Greek soldiers were very close friends with Albanian soldiers and would report those who attempted to flee the country. There was no room for error as the smallest mistake could end my life.

I also had to make sure that nothing suspicious was left behind. If the police had to go into my house to investigate, I didn't want them to find anything that might send my brother in prison. Albanian law enforcement officers didn't need much to make an arrest. I decided that I would wear nice clothes when I leave my home to fool passersby into believing that I was going somewhere nearby for fun. The clothes had to be dark so the soldiers on the mountains couldn't easily see me. As the day drew closer to depart I was still maintaining distance from my friends, while exercising and doing a lot of thinking.

At the beginning of November the weather forecasts in Albania and Greece predicted three to four days of heavy rain, mild temperatures, with little to no snow. This was the perfect weather to make my break. When I heard that I was overcome by emotions. After such a long wait I could hardly believe that my chance to escape had finally come. I was now on the brink of doing the craziest thing in the world.

A few days before my escape attempt was to begin something happened. I was walking home alone from work around midnight. While passing by the police station I noticed a truck parked right in front of the building. I could clearly see two bodies hanging from the back of the truck. Such a sight terrified me as I froze in fear. I knew I would be punished if I were caught, so I rushed to hide behind a nearby tree.

ACTING BEYOND MEASURES

"Thinking is easy, acting is difficult, and to put one's thoughts into action is the most difficult thing in the world."—Johann Wolfgang von Goethe

Two law enforcement officers came out of the station, each of them carrying a shovel. They walked toward the truck, cursing the dead bodies all the while. One of officers inched closer to the dead bodies as a shovel violently hits one of the corpses. The hit cut the corpse in half, while the offending officer continued to curse, seemingly unfazed by what he was doing. I could hardly believe what I was seeing.

I had heard so many terrible stories and had witnessed the cruelty of the communists, but I had never seen anything like this; and never this close. I didn't want to continue watching, but I had no choice. I had to remain in hiding until everything was safe for me to continue my walk.

It was very shocking to see what the law enforcement officers were doing to people, even to those who had already passed. It was even scarier for me to witness this just days before my escape. I didn't know who the victims were, but for the moment I thought that maybe they were prisoners who had died and were being transported for burial.

The next morning I learned that three citizens tried to escape and were caught. One of them was sent to a hospital in a critical condition and the other two were brutally killed. Hearing news like this could be very sobering and possibly deter someone from making an attempt to flee, but the brutality exhibited by the officers only strengthened my resolve to move ahead with my plan.

I was truly affected by what I'd witnessed, and honestly, I allowed my anger and disgust motivate me onward. I was no longer afraid of death. I was fully aware that my plans would be considered insane and I was no longer afraid of the risks involved. At this time I knew that there was only one option for Vladimir Gjini: freedom!

There is no price too high to pay for one's freedom. I thought to myself, "What sort of life could I possibly have without freedom? Without freedom there is no living; only constant survival." I had survived in Albania long enough to know that I could no longer continue in such an inhumane experience.

As soon as I heard that the weather had taken a turn for the worse, I had to successfully undertake my first act of defiance against the regime. To set my plan in motion I needed "permission" from the government to leave my hometown, Gjirokaster, and make my way to Partizani. Partizani, the border town from which I would make my escape, is a highly restricted area. My presence there would invariably raise suspicions on the part of the security forces and the sinister web of other communist party authorities.

I planned to let them know that I was there to attend a wedding, hoping that if I waited until the last possible moment it would keep the authorities from fully checking out my story. It was a huge risk, but it was one I had to take knowing that if I were denied for any reason my escape would be set back for an entire year while waiting for November to come again. As it were, the weather in November provided the best opportunity for such a daring escape. Nevertheless, I had to take the risk, and hopefully avoid getting caught in a lie by the security forces. The very next day, I went to the police station to apply for permission to travel.

Since one of my army friends lived in Partizani, I told the officer at the gate that he invited me to his wedding and I needed permission to participate. The office opened at 8:30 in the morning when they started accepting applications. After completing and filing the application they immediately let you know whether your application had been approved or declined. If your application was declined, you were done for the day; if it was approved, you had to go back around 1:00 PM to pick up the permission slip to travel.

I was hoping that they would not contact my friend to verify the information I had entered on my application. I felt comfortable within myself that they would not contact him, because there was not enough time for them to do so in person, and few families owned a phone. Moreover, even if he did have a phone, he was probably at work.

If they found out that I was lying to them, I would face serious consequences. When I arrived that morning, the police officer on duty at the office happened to be one of my neighbors. He helped me get in without waiting in line; introduced me to the authorities as a cousin of Rashide, and told them that I was applying for permission to attend a wedding in Partizani, a village of Saranda. He told them that I was a good neighbor, which helped to greatly expedite my application.

Together, these various factors (as well as a healthy dose of luck) helped me secure the much-needed permission that day. I had successfully overcome my first hurdle by gaining the State's permission to travel to Partizani. Soon I will be departing from my home with a heavy heart and deep sense of dread, eased only by my determination to taste freedom. I knew my goodbyes would be permanent and equally concerned about the fates of the family members I left behind—loved ones I would never see again. After formally receiving travel permission, I still had enough time to make it to work by 3 PM that day.

All the while, I had to be very careful to hide the permission slip from everyone I knew, even family members. During my last three nights at home, I slept with my socks on so I could hide the slip between my foot and the sock, because I had to make sure it was with me at all times.

My family couldn't know. I wasn't afraid that my brother or my sister-in-law would report me, but I was sure they would try to stop me if they learned about my deadly plan. They loved me, and knew full well the dangers of trying to cross the border: there was a very small chance of me actually making it to Greece alive.

As I was preparing to leave, I tried to sleep as much as possible so I would have energy for the days to come. It was impossible: too many thoughts were going through my mind. I kept thinking about my brother and everyone else I would never see again. To refocus my thoughts I kept repeating all the steps of my escape plan. I kept thinking of being captured, beaten, and shot.

I selected November 11, 1987 as my freedom day for a couple of reasons. First, the weather was predicted to be severe. Second, on November 8, 1941, The Communist Party of Albania (PKSH) was formed. In Albania, a few days before and after the holidays, the army was on high alert. During this period of high alert, soldiers had to serve long hours protecting the borders. I chose November 11th because that was the first night following high alert.

Having served in the army, I knew the soldiers would be exhausted from serving consecutive days on high alert. As a result, they would be less alert. The night before my escape, I told my family I would be going to Saranda the following morning to buy some lemons and olives for us. I also told them that I would stay there overnight, making sure they weren't going to wait up for me. As soon as I said this, my brother pulled me aside and questioned me. He knew right away I wanted to escape.

He pleaded desperately with me, telling me not to go through with my plan. He told me that they would certainly capture and kill me. Hearing this, I acted as though I didn't know what he was talking about. It had been a long time since we last talked about escaping. The only attitude I could have was to remain calm and attempt to convince him that I wasn't trying to escape. My brother already knew that I was going to try it one day; he just didn't know when. With all my trying and excuses, I don't think he believed a word I said to him.

That night I wanted to turn in to bed early, even though I knew I wasn't going to be able to sleep. As I was lying down, my brother and sister-in-law came into my room and started talking to me about a girl they knew from town. They kept me up till midnight trying to convince me to get engaged to her. I gave them excuses, telling them that was too early for me to start a family. They kept insisting, but after a while I told them that it was late; that we could finish our conversation at another time. I assured my brother that we would talk again. That night ended up being my third in a row without sleep. I spent all night replaying every move in my head. To overcome my fears I kept telling myself over and over again that I would make it. This was one of the most difficult part of my escape: encouragement. Since I didn't have anyone with whom I could safely share my plan, concerns, fears, and emotions, I had to quickly learn how to become my own motivator. If there would be anyone patting me on the back, telling me how well things will turn out, it would have to be me.

The morning of November 11, 1987, I got up, shaved, took a shower, and dressed in dark colors as I had planned. I took a bag with me, supposedly "to carry the olives and lemons" for my family. In reality, this bag was to serve as was my lifeline and inventory case.

Inside the bag I carried a small knife and a thin rope, about two meters long. I planned to buy some additional items once I arrived safely in Saranda. A few days before my escape I went to the bank to withdraw the money I had been saving up to this point. I took some with me, and left the rest in a place where my brother and sister-in-law would easily find it. I wanted them to have access to as much cash as possible since I would no longer be there to contribute financially to the household. Not to mention, I knew that my escape would lead the government to confiscate everything they owned.

I knew that dark times lay ahead and my path would be filled with danger. Therefore, before leaving the house I prayed to God for wisdom and to lead me along a safe path and guide my steps. That morning, my brother got up early too. I looked at his freshly face, which appeared slightly swollen from sleep. I took my time and carefully studied his countenance, knowing that this would be the last time I would see my beloved brother rise with the sun.

I kissed him goodbye as if I were going on a day trip, but within the depths of my broken heart I knew this was the last time I would see him. Can you imagine leaving your own house; your own family; knowing that you will never see them again? I left knowing that whomever and whatever I left behind would never see me again.

I left the house around 7:00 in the morning with thoughts of my family weighing heavily on my mind. From that moment on everything would be new and unfamiliar. I went downtown to have a cup of coffee,

then left the shop around 7:30 AM, walking toward the
bus station. On my way there, I met my friend Mihal.
Since I didn't report to work the day before he was
surprised to see me.

Citing the bad weather and the fact that I had
missed work the previous day, he thought I had escaped
already. I explained that I didn't go to work the day
before because I wasn't feeling well. Not wanting to
waste any time, I told him I had to catch the bus and said
our goodbyes. As I boarded the bus my journey to
freedom had begun! I thought about how the smallest
mistake could mean the end of my life, and about law
enforcement officers interrogating my family. I had to
quickly snap out of that negative thinking and encourage
myself to focus on a happier, brighter future.

As I was boarding, my brother got on, too.
Apparently, he had been following me all along. He saw
that I met Mihal, and he thought for sure I was trying to
escape with him. Since Mihal didn't board the bus with
me it might have confused my brother. Nevertheless, I'm
not sure what he thought when he saw us going in
different directions, but I knew for sure he didn't trust
me. He said he came on the bus to check if Mihal was
traveling with me.

Whispering, I told him to watch what he said. After confirming that Mihal wasn't on the bus, he began to relax. We kissed goodbye again, and he finally got off. I was seated near the window, which was rolled down. He approached my window and warned me again not to do anything insane. He remained at the station until the bus departed to make sure that Mihal wasn't getting on.

Whether Mihal got on or not, I knew that my brother was convinced that I was up to something. When the bus finally started moving, I looked at my brother for the last time with tears welling up in my eyes. I kept my eyes fixed out the window, not wanting people to see me crying. The trip to Saranda was roughly two hours, but it felt very short. I tried to savor every memory of my Albanian life, as hard as it was. I wanted to hold onto the feeling of my family's love forever. I wanted to always remember the beauty of my country, and to fill my lungs one last time with the air of my hometown.

As soon as we arrived in Saranda, I immediately bought my ticket for the second leg of my bus trip. I had to travel from Saranda to Partizani, which was located approximately 90 minutes away by bus. If I were driving a car I'm certain that I would make it in half that time. For one thing, I wouldn't have to stop to pick up and drop off passengers; it would be a straight ride. Unfortunately, the bus was my only option and it was already going according to plan.

With a little time to kill after purchasing my ticket, I stopped at a restaurant to eat. It was important that I kept up my energy to carry me through the day. From this moment forward there would be many unknowns. I didn't know the next time I would eat; what I was about to go through; if I was going to make it to Greece and, if I did; what was going to happen to me when I arrived there.

After eating as much as I could, I visited a convenience store to purchase some items that I would need for my escape. I planned to pick up some mandarins, lemons, cigarettes, a lighter, and some sugar. I bought about ten packs of cigarettes, because I smoked at the time. I also bought a lighter, because matches are no longer useful when they are wet.

I needed the mandarins for food (as well as for the water they contained), and sugar for emergency energy. My reasons for buying lemons was a bit more complicated; let me explain. I had to be prepared for the army's highly-trained attack K-9 units in case the rain stopped. The K-9s were very fast and aggressive. If I heard dogs coming, I would cut the lemons in half and squeeze the juice on my footprints. The acidic scent would keep them off my trail long enough to gain an advantage. The lemons were my only countermeasure for arguably the most dangerous threat to my escape.

After purchasing my bus ticket, dining and shopping, I had used up what little money I had brought with me, except for a few Albanian currency, which I wanted to keep as a memento. That afternoon, I boarded the bus departed Saranda around 1 PM. On the ride to Partizani I really began to feel the gravity of my situation. As we got closer, an enormous pressure began to build in me. That night, there could only be two outcomes: either I made it safely to Greece, or I'm shot by Albanian soldiers.

I tried to calm myself down as I didn't want to appear suspicious as we approached a checkpoint. It seemed as though everyone on the bus except me was from the area, and knew each other. I was the only stranger; the odd man out. They even dressed differently, so I really stood out. Thus, I had to remain extremely calm and behave nonchalant.

Two officers came on the bus and checked everyone's identification. All Albanians had to have their passports on them at the time, because they were used primarily as our photo IDs. When it was my turn, the officer checked my passport and saw I was from Gjirokaster. Staring at me intently, he asked for my permission to travel. He was trying to read my face, scanning for signs of nervousness. However, I had been preparing for this moment. There was no fear on my face. Eventually, the officer handed back my permission slip and left. YES! I had just overcome another hurdle.

When we arrived in Partizani, I stepped off the bus and took a quick smoke break. I didn't want to stay in that village for too long. Soon after, I started walking in the direction of Grazhdan, another village about an hour away by foot. It would be there that I would actually begin my escape. In that area, I was able to walk on the streets without fear.

Once I left Partizani, my permission slip would no longer be valid. Every action outside of this village would be illegal. Everything past that area would be a matter of life and death. As I made my way through the village I could tell that the residents eye me suspiciously. As far as they were concerned, I was either visiting someone or an escapee. At least that's what I would expect had it been me watching a total stranger meandering down our street. In this village, strangers were very uncommon. Knowing that my presence attracted unwanted attention, I tried to walk at a steady pace, hoping to avoid getting pulled into any conversation. As difficult as it was in this situation, I had to exude a sense of confidence that, in and of itself, may have caused further suspicion. My body language had to show that I knew where I was going, that I wasn't a stranger lost in the area. Yet, since I was actually a stranger and no one had ever seen me there before, it was critical that I got out quickly and safely without further concern. After passing through the village, I began walking through the hills, which meant that I was breaking the law.

Getting off the main road was critically important to protect myself on my dangerous journey. Yet, it also meant that my chances of seeing people would be little to non-existent. Even the distant sight of another human could help to make a person in my situation feel slightly less isolated, but in this case the isolation was exactly what I needed. My sense of loneliness caused me to smoke to keep myself busy and moving in the right direction. Smoking had become my best friend.

I burned through cigarette after cigarette to keep myself calm. I smoked extra during the day since I knew as much as enjoyed smoking, I couldn't continue to do so during the night. Surprisingly, I continued walking through the hills, I started passing a lot more people than I'd anticipated. Most of them were headed to the same bus station in Partizani which I had recently left.

As I walked rain started to fall, then pour. Luckily I had my umbrella to keep dry and hide my face. The time had come to minimize all eye contact to limit any chance that anyone would notice that I wasn't from around there. When I arrived at the top of the hill between Partizani and Grazhdan, I saw a small cave between the rocks. I decided to stop at the cave for a short time, because I needed to fix my bag. Up to this moment, I had to carry my bag as a handbag. In Albania, it was common for soldiers to carry backpacks, while everyone else carried bags in their hands. If anyone had seen me carrying a backpack before this point they would automatically assume that I was an escapee.

While in the cave I grabbed two rocks of similar size and weight, and placed them at the bottom of my bag; one in each corner. Then, I tied the corners containing the rocks with the rope I had taken from home. Finally, I made a loop with the rest of the rope hanging from the bag to tie it off so I could use it as a backpack. This was one of those moments when I was thankful for my service in the army, where I learned these and other survival skills.

I was enjoying a cigarette while preparing my bag, and then suddenly I heard footsteps that caused me to immediately stop. Looking onto the road I could see a familiar face. He lived in Grazhdan; the village where I served during my final months in the army. I had seen him many times before as I left the base. I also remembered him for a rather ironic reason: one of his family members had escaped years ago. In communist Albania, if someone from your family escaped, everyone else knew you as the family member of a criminal. He was carrying an 18-month old baby and coming towards me. He stopped and asked the dreaded question:

"What are you doing here"? Calmly, I answered, "Good evening, sir." He asked again. He also asked where I was going, knowing that I wasn't from the area. I told him that I was just trying to get out of the rain and take a smoke break. I told him, right off the bat, that I wasn't doing what he thought I was doing.

"My name is Vladimir Gjini," I continued. "And I know you; you are from Grazhdan. I served in the army there some time ago, but I see you don't remember me. I can't blame you for that, as I was always in uniform then. But, now you see me in casual clothes."

I continued engaging him in conversation, carefully explaining that I was going to Grazhdan to see my army friends. I also told him I was going to see my cousin Vlad, the top officer there. In the meantime, I showed him my permission slip, which was no longer valid. When I showed him the permission slip, I kept it far enough away so he wouldn't be able to read it clearly. I just needed him to believe what I was saying.

With a smile on my face, I then calmly asked him how he was doing. He then apologized for his suspicious attitude and for asking questions. He said that there were a lot of "unpleasant people" around, so he had to ask. I jokingly asked him if he thought I was really an escapee, and he laughed. After that, he told me to have a good night and left. That was obviously an enormous relief. Once again, I had managed to overcome another treacherous hurdle—and an unexpected one, at that. My prayers were definitely being answered, because that encounter could have turned out very differently and my

journey would have been severely cut short—
permanently!

Once he was out of sight I finished prepping my
bag and started walking toward Grazhdan. I walked very
slowly when no one was around, because I wanted to
pass some time until it became dark. Even as I walked
slowly there was always the fear that I would draw
attention. It was very risky. Even after I slowed down, it
seemed as though time was crawling and the sun's light
remained visible. It wasn't getting dark enough for me to
get away from the road and start climbing the mountain.

I started to become nervous, thinking that my
slow pace was probably not the greatest idea. For one
reason, the soldiers who carried binoculars might spot
me and find my movements suspicious. With that
thought I started walking faster. As soon as I knew that I
was out of the soldiers' line of sight I started walking in
the direction of Saranda. Then, I turned again toward
Grazhdan. Essentially, I kept pacing back and forth,
while coming very close to my escape territory, just to
pass time for darkness to set in. While I was walking
towards Grazhdan for the second time, I noticed it was
getting darker.

Next, I heard voices with unfamiliar accents, causing me to suspect the presence of soldiers. If I was discovered it would be a disaster, because my permit did not grant me approval to be in that area. I ran and hid behind some bushes. Understandably, I was terrified. I had no idea who they were or why they were there. As they passed, I heard them talking about me.

I heard one of them ask the other, "Where is that guy? We were supposed to meet him somewhere around here. From the time the other guy called, he was supposed to be in Grazhdan."

His companion said, "Let's walk further down, and then we'll go back to the base." When I heard them talking, I knew that the man I met in the cave had reported me, and that they were soldiers sweeping the area. From these soldiers' calculations, I should've arrived in Grazhdan a while back.

There was an area on the mountain where anyone who wanted to escape had to pass. It was considered an impossible route. To the left of the mountain was a cliff, and to the right was the army base. To climb down the cliff was incredibly dangerous and time-consuming, so that option was out. The best option at that moment was to run to the base of the mountain and start climbing.

Normally, as soon as it became dark, the soldiers headed to that location to secure it because of its appeal to potential escapees. I had to pass through before the soldiers arrived; I didn't have time to waste. I wasn't sure when the soldiers who walked past me would report that I wasn't anywhere to be found. As soon as they did, soldiers would rush to seal off my escape point.

As soon as they were out of sight, I slung my bag tightly around my shoulders and started running toward the mountain. After running for around 10 minutes, I fell into a canal that was about five feet deep. My left leg and body fell into the canal, but my right leg remained twisted out on top. I felt excruciating pain radiating from my right knee. I groaned in agony and pulled my right leg inside the canal. Feeling my knee with my hands, I realized that I had dislocated it. I was in agonizing pain, but I wasn't even thinking about it; I couldn't walk.

To turn around and go back home, I had to walk a very long way. I had no idea how long it would take for me to walk to Greece from this point, either. I didn't know what to do, but I started by dragging myself out of the canal. I didn't have time to waste; I needed to make a decision.

The area where I dislocated my knee.

CONFLICT OF THE MIND

"If you want something you have never had, you must be willing to do something you have never done."—Thomas Jefferson

At that moment, as I sat on the ground with a dislocated knee, I told myself I would never go back. Even in my condition, I truly believed I could make it, no matter the obstacle. Deep within myself, I knew that I would never have another opportunity like this. However, to move forward, I first had to figure out what I was going to do about my knee. I tried to push my kneecap back into place, but I couldn't. It was too painful, and I couldn't risk making any noise.

From that moment on I had to be as stealthy as possible, since any unnecessary noise could easily compromise my position and put my escape in jeopardy. In the dark I had no idea if soldiers were around. Then I thought of a possible solution: if two trees were close together, I could place my foot in one and force my weight onto the other - that might be enough to pop my knee cap back into place. I started looking around, and I soon noticed a few small trees about 20 yards from where I was; I dragged myself there. There was a tree which separated in the middle into a "V" shape, and another regular tree next to it. I found what I was looking for.

I placed my injured leg into the "V" of the split tree and pushed myself securely between the opposing tree for leverage. I needed to lock my knee, while using my arms to pull my body back and forth several times until the knee popped back into place. It was unbelievably painful; I'm not sure I could ever endure that kind of pain again. Worst of all I couldn't make any noise. I didn't have any other option at that time, so I kept pushing until my knee popped back into place. I was still in tremendous pain afterwards, so I rested for about five minutes to regain feeling, composure, and energy.

When I tried to walk again, I realized I still couldn't put much weight on my leg. I ended up dragging my right leg for a good part of the journey so I could keep moving. I hoped that the more I used my injured leg, the more likely I'd be able to walk and distribute my weight on it. So that's what I did. Of course, I was concerned of causing permanent damage to my kneecap. When all things were considered, I figured that it was better to lose my leg than to lose my life. With that resolved I kept walking toward Greece.

After about 20 minutes of walking, the pain in my leg begun to subside. That was a good and welcome sign. It motivated me to pick up my pace. Fear and determination helped to numb a lot of the pain in my right leg. Thankfully, my brain prioritized survival over the pain from my leg as I soldiered on. The more I walked, the more confident I became. I soon forgot about my knee altogether and focused instead on getting back on the road, which is where I needed to be. I started climbing as quickly as I could.

After a few minutes, I heard horses walking and breathing heavily below me. I wasn't sure if the horses heard my footsteps when I passed through, but they were spooked and started walking. I immediately stopped, thinking that if there were horses around, then a shepherd would be nearby.

Sometimes, the shepherds carried firearms to protect themselves, or fire in the air to signal for soldiers. The rocks on the mountain looked solid, but they easily crumbled under my weight when I stepped on them. That made my escape much harder. Now, my best hope was that the pouring rain would help mask my footsteps. I started walking very slowly, looking around and trying to listen for noises to analyze what they were and where they were coming from. It was very dark, raining, the fog had fallen, and visibility was very poor.

I noticed a small cabin in front of me and realized there was a great chance a shepherd was inside. I stopped again and looked around for a safe place to pass without being seen. However, the only reasonable path led directly in front of the cabin's door. Very slowly, I crept along one side of the cabin, checking if there was a path that didn't require me to pass the entrance. The walls were built with rocks, but the fourth wall didn't have a door, however, there was a fairly large opening.

I looked through the opening and noticed the shepherd sitting by the fire. He had placed a piece of metal on top of the fire to cover it from the rain as the cabin had no roof. His head was bobbing up and down, but every so often he would open his eyes. I couldn't go around the back either, because the cabin was built on the edge of a cliff.

I turned around and looked at the shepherd again. He kept opening and closing his eyes. Staring through the hole, I prayed he would fall asleep so I could creep past the front unnoticed. But, it was taking too long and I was running out of time. Suddenly, I thought of a brilliant idea. I bent over, touching my palms to the ground, and sliding them across the ground until my chest and stomach were flat to the ground. Then, I glided my body across the other side of the opening, while dragging my feet behind. Next, I used my muscles to lift my feet and hands back onto my bent-over position, lifted my body, and stood upright. Essentially, I dragged myself like a caterpillar and it worked.

It felt great to overcome another obstacle. If the shepherd had seen me I might have had to attack him with my knife and possibly choose my life over his. However, my goal was to make it across the border without shedding any blood. I thanked God and kept going.

I continued walking very slowly knowing that the shepherd's dog was probably nearby keeping watch over the horses and sheep. My hair bristled with a sense of danger. There were many small rocks at this particular location on the mountain, so I had to walk carefully to avoid making any noise. If I climbed too quickly the small rocks would slide down the slope and make a racket. By this time the rain had stopped, so there was nothing to camouflage sounds of my movement. After

20 minutes or so, I passed through the area with a slight deviation from my originally planned route. I tried to imagine the map of the terrain as though I was holding it in front of me, and I climbed more to the right of the mountain. It was very difficult to see where I was going due to extreme darkness and clouds obscuring the top of the mountain.

The area where I was climbing at that time was comprised mostly of gravel from erosion, and the rocks were still rolling down from the mountain. I didn't know on which side of the mountain the soldiers were located, and the terrain and weather weren't helping much, either. Sometimes, I had sharp pain in my right knee, causing me to constantly worry about twisting one of my ankles. I bit my lip to stifle my own groans of agony. It took more than three hours to pass that area.

After I had gotten past that section of the mountain, the ground became more solid, thus making climbing easier and less noisy. I tried to make up some of the time I had lost before. It also started pouring again, so I decided to run for a bit. Unfortunately, I ran into something unexpected. There were two wires: one was a foot above the ground, and the other a couple of feet above it. I tripped and fell on the top wire. I still don't know where the wires were coming from or what they were tied to, since they were in the air when I ran through them.

I felt one wire touching my legs, and another touching my hips. While moving the wires with my body I heard a noise like the shaking of soda cans filled with rocks, coming from the ends of the wires. Clearly, someone had taken time to set a trap to be alerted of uninvited guests in the area, and I had unknowingly triggered the alarm. I was worried that someone might've heard the rattling cans, but thankfully the heavy rain was louder than the cans. I got up and saw that I was on the edge of a cliff. Again, I thanked God.

At that point, I was able to see the top of the mountain, and I immediately knew I was headed in the right direction. After about 30 minutes of running and climbing, I saw a pathway probably about a foot and half wide—that was the pathway the soldiers walked to protect the mountain. I knew that there was a chance I would run into soldiers if I used their path, but I also knew I would save an enormous amount of time by taking the risk. In the end, I got on the path and started running, trying to take in all of my surroundings. During my run, I heard someone spit.

I stopped, laid down, and looked around. I didn't see or hear anything for about a minute. Then, I stood up, but I didn't move. I couldn't see anything. Then I looked down, and four-five feet across from me I saw legs. It was a soldier sitting on a rock inside a small cave. I guessed he was trying to find shelter from the rain. He was sitting exactly where I was trying to pass through. I saw a machine gun nestled between his legs. He was right in front of me. This was the closest I came to being spotted, and even killed. I knew that there was a chance that I could be discovered by taking the soldiers' path, but I could never in my wildest dreams imagine that I'd wind up within a few feet of the enemy.

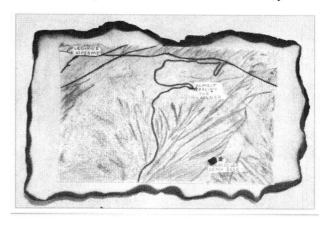

The area where I came within 4-5 feet of the soldiers.

My heart was racing. Normally, soldiers patrol in groups of three and stay within 10 meters of each other. Typically, they tie a string to their wrists, which connects to the wrists of the other soldiers in their squad. If they need help, they communicate with each other by pulling the string. For example, pulling it once could mean, "Be careful, I heard something," and pulling it twice could mean, "I need help."

I didn't know what to do, but I had to make a quick decision. If I hurt him he would probably make noise or pull the string and the other soldiers would kill me very easily. However, there really was no way around him. To head up or down meant scaling a very steep cliff. If I didn't see a soldier and tried to scale past him, he wouldn't even need his weapon to execute me.

A simple push would send me tumbling hundreds of feet down the mountain to certain death. I finally decided to turn around. I moved away from the soldier with extreme caution. With our proximity, even the rain wouldn't mask my steps. I was very concerned that even the sound of my heavy breathing could be heard and reveal my position. I walked backwards very slowly, making sure not to disturb any rocks. When I was about a hundred meters from the soldier, I started scaling the cliff.

It was the middle of the night, so I could hardly see what I was grabbing onto. The rocks on that cliff were fragile, and many times when I grabbed a rock to pull myself up, it broke. I quickly grabbed for branches near me to slow down. I knew that a single slip-up would send me plummeting to my death. I spent nearly an hour scaling that cliff, constantly frightened for my life.

All of my muscles were burning intensely; I was covered with cuts and bruises from the rocks and branches. The rocks were very sharp, and my skin was soft and wrinkled from hours of being in the rain. I couldn't see the blood, but I could feel warm streaks running down my arms and my legs. However, the fear of dying easily trumped whatever pain I was experiencing at that moment. I never stopped.

When I got to the top of the cliff, I sat down for a couple of minutes to catch my breath. Up to that moment, I hadn't actually bothered to check the time. I had an old watch with me, so I decided now would be a good time: it was 3:30 AM. I knew I had a long way to go, and I also knew I soon wouldn't have the cover of darkness on my side. I was ecstatic to have made it to the top of the cliff, and past the soldiers. At this time, one of my biggest obstacles was behind me. One cannot imagine how relieved I was to put those soldiers far behind me. Even though I didn't know what the rest of my escape would bring, I didn't have the fear of losing my life at the hands of Albania soldiers any longer.

Of course, I still had to be careful. In Albania, circumstances could change at any moment. After overcoming the cliff, large, solid rocks dominated the terrain. I continued climbing the mountain for about half a mile, then stopped to make sure I was going in the right direction. I looked around and realized I had passed the white strip which I had seen on the mountain during my army days. It was about three meters wide, and I probably missed it when I climbed the cliff. That was the only area where they couldn't paint the rocks.

Knowing that I had passed the soldiers I decided to turn around and check it out. I walked back about 300 meters and, for the first time, saw the white strip from up close. I didn't want to touch it with my hand, because I didn't know what it was. I stepped on the white strip and felt a crunch. It felt as though I was crushing a rock. To this day, I'm not sure whether the strip consisted of a trail of white rocks, or if they had simply painted over the ground.

However, the crunching sound was quite loud, so I stopped being curious and turned around. Walking back in the right direction, I realized I should probably eat something. I had lost a lot of energy. I cut a hole in my bag and grabbed a mandarin. I peeled the skin and placed it back in my bag, since I didn't want to leave anything behind. I enjoyed my mandarin while walking towards the top of the mountain.

Every step I took brought me closer to my goal and whatever pain may have lingered in my body soon became a faint memory. My future was getting closer and closer with every step up that mountain and I was determined to get there. I could sometimes see the mountaintop, but only when the clouds permitted. I was trying to follow my intended path, because that was the shortest route. At that moment, no matter which direction I was headed, I was going to make it to the top. I couldn't wait to get to the other side. After climbing for an hour or so, I reached the very top of the mountain!

This was it. After so long, the end of my mission was in sight. I went down on my knees and thanked God for helping me overcome every obstacle I had encountered. I had an intense feeling of euphoria and I was beyond grateful to accomplish my goal. All night I climbed rocks, cliffs, and an impossibly difficult terrain. The top of the mountain was littered with rocks and dirt. As I arrived I stepped on dirt for the first time after hours and hours of struggling over rocks, gravel, rain, and soldiers. It was a jolt of relief that I stepped on the dirt.

I felt safer when I reached the top and didn't feel the difficulties of the night. I knew the top of the mountain was the border of Albania and Greece. My excitement overshadowed the pain and suffering I had experienced—not just during my escape, but every single day, month, and year while living under the most difficult challenges in Albania. It is impossible to explain the scope of the feelings in those moments. The feelings of standing on the top of the mountain knowing that anything is achievable are indescribable. Right there on the top, I experienced unrivaled feelings of accomplishment and I couldn't feel pain or exhaustion. I felt energized, relived, and like I had been born again.

I began my descent. Climbing the mountain was extremely difficult, but going down was even worse. I had seen the mountain many times from the Albanian side, but I had no idea what awaited me on the other side. Another mountain was next to it, which blocked even more moonlight and further obscured my vision. The terrain changed again. The rocks became slippery and slimy in some places. I stopped on the edge of a big rock and tried to look for a less dangerous route. While scanning the area I felt a big piece of the rock begin to crack where I was standing. That's when I realized that I was standing at the edge of the cliff.

The area where I had to seek a safe route down the mountain.

The rock gave way under me. I jumped and grabbed one of the few branches within reach. That moment crushed my euphoria. I realized that the danger wasn't yet behind me, and if I didn't act quickly, I would fall down the cliff and die. Foolishly, I had gotten carried away by my excitement and had forgotten that a small mistake could ruin everything I had endured and all my carefully laid plans for the future.

I collected myself and began to move more slowly, though I ached to race towards my destination. By now it felt as though I was merely dragging myself along, holding onto rocks, bushes—anything within reach. The rock-face was very slippery and I could hear water coming from above like a waterfall. I slid from a particularly slippery rock and almost fell down the cliff, again. I calmed my pounding heart, gathered my strength, and lifted myself up to find a different path.

After descending about another two hundred meters, I realized that I was dealing with extremely tough terrain. At that very moment, I heard footsteps thudding against rocks and rocks rolling down. I knew it had to be the soldiers with their K-9 units. I tried to calm my nerves and think logically about what could be done to avoid my would-be captors. Luckily, there was a tree nearby. I hid behind the trunk of that tree on the side facing Greece to avoid being seen. Based on the information they received earlier from the gentleman I met in the cave, they were probably still searching for me. I was furious. Why did the Albanian soldiers have to follow me this far? I had been on Greek land for at least the last mile.

I was very still. Of all my five physical senses, I could only rely on my hearing for the time being. I had to be extra cautious and quiet until I was safe again. As I hid behind the trunk of the tree, my ears strained to catch any hint that they neared. Standing there, still so far from freedom, I reached into my bag and grabbed a few lemons. I started cutting them in half to have them ready in case I needed to rub lemon against my shoes. Hopefully, this would throw off the dog's sense of smell. Then again, if I heard the dogs approaching the area where I was standing it would be better to climb the tree: the knife and lemons were not powerful enough to defend against a K-9 unit. Or maybe it would be best if I stood still and waited for dawn to arrive.

At this point, every decision carried tremendous weight and it was difficult to make up my mind. There was no time to waste, therefore I had to make a quick decision. I knew that the terrain was extremely dangerous, so I decided to wait for a while.

While waiting behind the tree until I was safe, I considered the safest move for the situation, while trying to discern what was going on around me. Eventually, I fell asleep while standing in the pouring rain in deep thought.

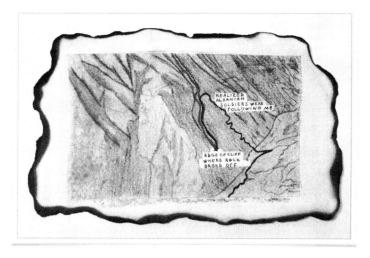

The area where I hid behind a tree (and fell asleep while standing) to avoid being seen by the soldiers.

It was the fourth night in a row that I had not closed my eyes for sleep. I had endured climbing of cliffs and all the mental and emotional pressure since I left the house the morning before. Finally, sleep overcame me. It was a mistake, but one I was unable to prevent. After 20 minutes or so, I felt rain dripping onto

my face and woke up. Upon waking, I shook off my
disappointment at the time lost and did my best to focus
on finding the best path forward.

I saw a building at the bottom of the mountain. I
wasn't sure if it was a Greek army base, so I had to be
careful about how I approached it. At this point in my
escape, I wasn't afraid of the Albanian soldiers anymore,
but I still had to be look out for Greek soldiers. I was no
safer around them than in the company of Albanian
soldiers. Greek soldiers were known to capture escapees
and return them to Albania. To avoid the soldiers, I
decided to go through the forest. Going through the trees
and creeks provided cover, which made it easier for me
to hide from soldiers.

The terrain was filled with slimy rocks, cliffs,
and a lot of water coming down from the top of the
mountain. It was the fourth day of heavy rain; and the
creeks were full to the point of flooding. The land was
slick with water from the heavy overflow. Moving
through the forest would be nearly as tiresome as
navigating the mountain, but at least I would see where I
was going and benefit from my other senses.

I descended slowly, holding onto the bushes
until I reached an area where I couldn't see the building

with the Greek soldiers anymore. I really needed a break, so I took advantage of that. I sat down for a cigarette and enjoyed the moment. It had been a long night, but I was also delighted to accomplish my dream after so many years. I was only thirteen when I first thought of escaping, and although it took me twelve years to realize my dream, I finally did it. I didn't know what life would bring me from that moment on, but I was ecstatic to have escaped Albania and its confinements. After I finished my cigarette, I moved on.

The most difficult part was going down the cliff. It wasn't that big, but without rope or any other assistance it was dangerous. I slid and was forced to scramble for a nearby branch to avoid what seemed like a continuous series of falls. Descending the mountain on the Greek side caused far more physical suffering than I had experienced while climbing the Albanian side. In Albania, I was distracted by my fear of the soldiers. Now that I was in Greece, their absence forced me to focus entirely on the physical strain I had experienced. I began descending the mountain around 4:30 AM, but it was around 11:30 AM when I was almost at the bottom.

As I approached the bottom of the mountain, I came across a brook about six meters wide. The level of the water was really high because of the rain. The water was rushing at a high-speed, and it was strong enough to carry large rocks and pieces of debris along for the ride. I wasn't worried about the rushing water, but the rocks were another matter entirely. There was very little I could have done to avoid slamming into rocks if the strong currents overpowered me.

I walked up and down along the side of the brook to see if I could find a spot that was narrow, but it was the same width at almost every point. I needed another way across, and after scanning the area further I found a spot where my side of the brook was higher than the other side.

I decided to jump from one side to the other side of the brook. I backed up, hoping to gain enough momentum and distance to jump clear across the brook. Unfortunately, my jump wasn't long enough to reach the other bank and I landed in the water. Thankfully, I landed close enough to the other bank where the water level was roughly two feet deep. While I was unable to avoid debris entirely, at least I wasn't severely injured.

I made it safely to the other side of the brook for yet another success on my incredible journey. Now that I had made it to the other side of the brook, a hill provided enough cover to ensure that whomever I had seen earlier near the building could not spot me. I took this opportunity to allow myself another short break.

My clothes were soaked from the rain and very dirty with mud and slime. I rested my backpack on the ground and proceeded to undress. I took off everything except my underwear. Next, I washed them briskly before putting them back on. My clothes were soaked again, but at least this time they were cleaner than before. Finally, I sat on a rock and ate four mandarins with some sugar since it had been a while since I had eaten.

I was really thirsty, but I didn't have water and couldn't drink from the brook, because it was full of debris. As I sat smoking I began to feel a pain in my right knee. It became increasingly painful, so much that I had a difficult time bending it. I was afraid of getting stuck there, knowing that I was still in danger, so I braced myself and moved on.

The road along which I walked was narrow and I thought that it might be a hunting area. I saw shells from a machine gun, empty soda cans, and other trash on the ground that could easily be associated with hunting activity. It was a strange sight, because we didn't have hunting grounds in Albania. The trash on the ground made me realize that I had actually escaped from my old life. From that moment on, my goal was to adjust to this new life—my escape from the dictatorial system. That case was over for me. I knew that my problems didn't end there, but the biggest challenge—escaping—had been accomplished.

I realized that the road led to the building that I had seen from far away. Even though I didn't know the purpose of building, I decided to walk in that direction. I didn't want to risk taking a different route and find myself back in Albania. When I got close to the building I tried not to walk on the main road anymore. Instead, I walked through the bushes and stopped on the side of the building. I saw a soldier who was dressed in a uniform that looked different from the Albanian uniform. This told me that I had arrived at a Greek base.

The Greek soldier marched carelessly in front of the building, facing the mountain. I needed a way around the building. The wide open space immediately behind the building wasn't an option, because the soldier would spot me with ease. The only alternative was a cliff, which was located right in front of me. The bushes there would provide adequate cover, but it would be extremely dangerous to climb. If I climbed the mountain, went around the cliff and descended again, it would take me probably three hours just to pass the building. Another challenge: I was unsure if that path would take me back into Albanian territory.

THE FIRST SIGNS OF FREEDOM

"My life is my message."—Mahatma Gandhi

I checked the front of the building for any possible way around it. At the front was a very steep cliff, and below was the brook that I had crossed earlier. This part of the brook had a lot more water than the spot where I crossed earlier. It was impossible for me to go through there.

My options were to either wait for the soldier to go inside to do something or wait until it got dark. As a former soldier I know that it was only a matter of time before it became necessary to leave his post. Whether it was to break for lunch, use the restroom, or leave entirely at the end of his shift. Sooner or later he had to go.

I decided to wait near the bushes as I kept an eye on the soldier, hoping that he'd soon disappear inside the building. After approximately 30 minutes, he went inside. That's when I quickly rushed to the corner of the building and waited there for nearly 30 seconds to make sure no one else was around. I knew I had to make my move now, as this was my best chance to get past the building without being seen. Otherwise, I would have to wait longer, increasing the likelihood of them killing me in the dark. I figured that if I was spotted in the afternoon, the chances of them returning me to Albania wasn't that high. I held onto that thread of hope. Then, I ran as fast as I could past the building.

I hid behind the bushes on the other side, taking a moment both to relish in this victory and to catch my breath. A minute or so afterwards, I saw the soldier come out again, this time eating something. I felt very lucky to have arrived around lunch. I continued walking through the bushes until I couldn't see the building anymore, doing my best to walk through the bushes parallel to the pathway. I didn't want to lose my sense of direction. I continued walking until I saw a village in the distance.

There was a paved road, which I assumed was a main road leading into the heart of Greece. In Albania, the roads in the villages that are close to the borders are left unpaved. This small detail further convinced me that I was heading toward Greece, and away from Albania.

By 1 PM I reached the village. Upon arrival I felt a lot more comfortable. This was the first time in many hours I didn't feel the need to hide my presence.

Although I still had to exercise caution, I felt that I could relax a little more.

I kept walking through the empty streets of the village in the pouring rain. On one side of the road was a church. It was the first time I had ever seen a church in real life. I realized I had begun a new life and gave thanks to God for giving me that opportunity. I was delighted to know that, from that moment on, I would be able to practice my religion freely. As I continued walking I reached an area where I could see the entire layout of the village. Exhausted, I followed the main road, hoping to head toward the cities.

At this time, I wanted nothing more than to find a cave, or anywhere with cover from the rain, in which to spend the night. I thought, perhaps I would find some sticks to build a fire, too.

I looked exhausted, my clothes were ripped all over, and I was soaking wet from walking so much in the rain. I passed a coffee shop and, though I walked right in front of the door, I didn't turn my head. I didn't want anyone to see me and recognize that I was a stranger. After I was about 50 feet away, I heard someone calling, trying to draw my attention. I turned around and saw an elderly woman. I didn't understand what she was saying, but I assumed she asked me where I was heading. Thinking quickly, I said Janina, the name of a town in Greece that was probably three hours away from where we were standing. I didn't know how to speak Greek, so I couldn't say more. I had learned a few Greek phrases, but mostly related to questions about myself and my family. I anticipated that these were the first questions the Greek authorities would ask me.

She continued speaking to me, and that time I understood her. She told me to come inside, but I wasn't sure what to do. I debated whether I should comply or run away. Then, I thought that running away wouldn't be a good idea, because they might call the authorities. I decided to follow her into the coffee shop. It was a very nice, beautiful and immaculate place. Once inside I immediately saw an elderly man sitting on a chair with a cane beside him.

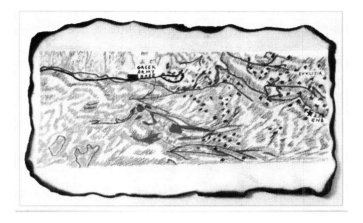

The area (star on the right) where I successfully ended my escape.

The woman started talking to me in Greek again, and I spoke in Albanian. Neither of us could understand each other, so most of the conversation was based on inferences. When she asked me a question and mentioned Albania, I assumed she had asked if I was from Albania and told her, "Yes", in Albanian. I hoped she would understand, because a lot of Albanians arrived in Greece and made it their home for a lack of better options. It didn't take long for them to realize that I had just escaped.

The old man must have been paying attention to the strained conversation between the old woman and me. He started talking to me, but with very little

Albanian. Perhaps, he was using a little of his Albanian to entice me to speak or make me feel more comfortable. Whatever his reason, it worked. I was thrilled to hear someone using even a few Albanian words, even though I had a difficult time understanding him, but I did when he asked me where I was from and some other simple questions. It was easier to understand each other after we found out that he also spoke Albanian.

The woman asked me if I wanted anything to eat or drink, and offered me anything I wanted. Since I wasn't very hungry at that moment, I politely refused their offer. The old man beckoned me to sit down, relax, and not to be afraid. He assured me that I was safe.

Between the two of them, they kept pushing me to eat something, no matter how many times I told them that I had already eaten a few mandarins earlier in the day. The woman felt heartbroken for me and insisted that I eat something. After a while, I felt obligated and accepted her offer by requesting a cup of coffee. I reached into my bag for my cigarettes, but the woman got a pack from her store and gave it to me. She gave me an unopened pack to keep and told me to save mine.

I put my cigarettes away and opened her pack. It was the first time I had ever smoked a cigarette from a different country. After she brought me the coffee, she told the man to explain to me that she would call secret services and for me not to be afraid because I was safe.

She wanted him to explain to me that they would take care of me and all I had to do was complete some paperwork in the Greek government's offices. This didn't surprise me. I was illegal in Greece and had been expecting to complete immigration paperwork. I thanked them for helping me and the woman went to make the phone call. Within 15 minutes, a tall, mustached gentleman in his mid-30s showed up at the door.

He approached me and extended his hand to shake mine. Then, he asked the old man to explain to me that after I finished my coffee I had to go with him to a government office to complete some paperwork. I didn't want him to have to wait for me, so I drank the coffee as quickly as I could.

As we drove in his jeep to the government office, I apologized in my language for sitting in his vehicle with wet clothes. I hoped that he understood what I was saying to him, but I was uncertain, because he didn't know Albanian and I didn't know Greek. After a while, he stopped at a building, which looked like a checkpoint station. There I saw six gentlemen in their forties, all in uniform. They tried to communicate with me, but I couldn't understand anything they were saying. The driver walked away for a moment, and after about 10 minutes he returned with a bundle of clothes in his hands.

At first, I thought he had gone to the store and purchased the clothes, but I later found out that the clothes were donated by a church. We went back in the vehicle and drove to a village called Filat, where his office was located. It was still raining, which made the cold temperatures persist. When I entered his office, I saw a stove in the corner of the room and marveled at how warm the room felt.

Next, he handed me the clothes from the church and told me to try them on and sit next to the stove. Most of our communication was carried out in the form of gestures. Then he walked out of the office to give me some privacy.

I took off my wet clothes and tried the clothes on. Surprisingly, almost all of them fit me very well. I had never owned a pair of jeans in my life because there were none in Albania. Since my body had been on the move for hours, I wasn't cold. I wore the jeans and a sweater, which felt undeniably comforting.

After a few minutes, the gentlemen that were standing by the gate came into the office and kept telling me to stay next to the stove. I spoke in Albanian, telling them that I wasn't cold, but they thought I didn't understand. All of them seemed to take sympathy on, so they put together whatever money they had in their pockets and handed it to me.

I didn't know the value of the money at the time, but they gave me 23,000 drachma. It was amazing how kindly they were treating me. This generosity would never have happened in Albania! Instead, a person would be quickly imprisoned for no reason. Yet, here in Greece it seems as though everyone I've met so far was willing to share their resources and make sure that my needs were met.

After about 30 minutes, a higher ranking officer stepped into the office. I didn't know who he was and why he was there, but I assumed he was someone important because everyone stood when he walked through the door. He said something to them and they moved me to a room with a big table in the middle. They told me to have a seat and wait. I started feeling a sharp pain in my knee, but I had to ignore it until later.

The driver who had brought me there walked in with two other gentlemen holding papers. One of them knew very little Albanian. They asked me where I was from; what my name was; my age—the basic questions. After they finished they told me that I had to wait there for a longer period of time as they were expecting three other individuals from the capital of Greece, Athens, to come and talk with me.

I was informed that when it was found out that someone had escaped from Albania, they left Athens in a helicopter. They were on their way and would arrive in approximately 30 minutes. The gentlemen told me that these individuals were in the secret service and that one of them was an Albanian translator. They were preparing me. I was told that when secret service arrived they would ask me many questions and urged me to be honest.

I couldn't understand if this intensity stemmed from their own experiences or if they were simply afraid of the secret services. It occurred to me that maybe other people who had escaped were dishonest because they were nervous and while trying to protect themselves. There was no reason for them to put so much emphasis on honesty with me. I didn't know what they were going to ask me, but I told them that I wasn't scared because I had nothing to hide.

While waiting for the secret services to arrive they offered me food and drink. It was definitely a kind gesture. Unfortunately, I didn't recognize the food they offered and selected pizza. That was my very first time eating pizza, and it was delicious, although I ate very little in the past 24 hours. Honestly, I was exhausted from so many days of stress and physical activity, and my body needed fluids more than food.

Around 4:30 in the afternoon the secret services and those who had interviewed me earlier entered the room. They sat around the table, opened their briefcases, and placed many documents before us.

First, they wanted a brief biography on me so they started with the same set of basic questions I'd already provided in my first interview. They asked for my full name; where I am from; how many members there were in my family; where I had grown up; where I went to school; where I worked. They wanted to know everything about my hometown, including where the stores were located; the school; the factory where I worked; who I knew from the town; and every detail about my life in Gjirokaster.

They were also very interested in knowing where the fuel stations and tanks were located. They asked where I had served; what kind of weapons we used; the size and manufacture of the weapons; how many people I knew from there; the names of the officers; the chief's name and physical appearance from where I spent my last months of service. Their questions led me to believe that they were mainly interested in the Albanian army.

Although I was emotionally and physically exhausted I had no choice but to comply with the seemingly never-ending questions. I even drew my old base for them, including as much detail as possible. I had to indicate where the weapons and munition supplies were located. I included the sleeping areas, kitchen, checkpoints, offices, and everything else that made up the army base. They repeated the same questions over and over, testing me to see if I would give them the same answers. I was certain and truthful in answering all the questions.

It was getting very late and I was getting to the point where I could no longer keep my eyes open. I had not slept for five days in a row, and my head was beginning to feel very heavy. Although I did my best to continue, I came to a realization where I simply couldn't remember what I was saying anymore.

Having sat for so long only contributed to the pain in my knee, which had worsened substantially. For hours I tried to keep my leg straight, but it soon became stiff to the degree that I could no longer bend it. After a certain time they realized that I was in some sort of discomfort. Perhaps it was a measure of pain in my face that gave away my worsening condition.

Not once during my interrogation did I complain about my injury until one of the gentlemen in the room asked if I was okay. I admitted that my knee was bothering me and explained that I had been injured early in my escape. I explained to them that I escaped in this condition, meaning it wasn't a pressing issue. He informed me that the following day they would bring a doctor to examine my knee. It was kind of him to say that, but I never saw a doctor during the time I spent there.

They went back to questioning and asked me to explain how I escaped from beginning to end. Not wanting to go into every intricate detail I decided to offer a condensed version of my ordeal. Based on the questions they asked, it seemed as though they needed to know everything about me; making sure that I was not a secret agent of the Albanian government. In retrospect I would probably have done the same thing if the roles were reversed.

As my interrogation was coming to a close they asked me if I had any questions or concerns, or if I needed anything. I didn't know the laws of the country and I didn't know what procedure they followed with refugees. If they had to notify Albanian government about my escape, I wanted them to give me at least a month before they notified the government. There were Albanian agents on the streets of Greece and I could fall prey to them at any time; if the government were notified, it would be at great personal risk to me.

I asked them for that favor, and after I explained my reasoning they assured me they would not say anything for a month. All communication went through the translator that night. During the conversation, however, I noticed that one of the gentlemen was nodding his head in agreement from time to time as if he understood what was being said. This head nodding occurred on various occasions, even before I was finished speaking. I had a strong feeling that he was fluent in Albanian all along.

Even though I was very tired, they continued questioning me until around 6:30 the next morning. Then they shook my hand and the translator told me to go into one of the rooms to get some sleep. He asked the men to provide me with blankets, while reassuring me not to worry, because I was safe there.

I went to the corner of one of the rooms, placing one blanket on the floor and using the other to cover myself. As I said, I was beyond exhausted, but equally excited about everything I had accomplished. Most of all I was proud of myself for remaining calm and grateful to have escaped and live to tell about it.

I had nothing more to give; nothing more to tell; and nothing to worry about. I had done everything that was asked of me and within a minute I was falling asleep. Not too long after drifting off to sleep I was awakened by the voices of the office personnel arriving for work that morning. I remember them saying to me "Siko, siko". I later learned that they were beckoning me to get up, but at the time I had no idea what they were saying. I was sleep deprived and wanted nothing but rest, but I had no choice to rise.

The nap was brief that I'd probably have been better off staying awake. By this time my knee was stiff and wouldn't bend much. Truth be told I was worried about the pain because I didn't know how severely my knee was injured. I asked one of the officers if they could give me some hot water and soap to massage my knee.

I hoped that the warm massage would help me regain some mobility in the leg for the day. I went to the restroom, sat on the floor, submerged my knee in the hot water, and started massaging it with soap. I massaged my knee for a while and did my best to walk on it afterwards. It wasn't healed, but it was bearable.

That was the first sunny day after many days of heavy rain. I went to stand on the balcony and noticed a church directly across from the building, and a school next to it. I watched the children walking to school and enjoying the fresh morning air. I cannot describe the feelings I experienced from waking up in a different country on such a gorgeous day. Knowing how many obstacles I had to overcome during my life in Albania, as well as the arduous trek across the mountains to freedom brought tears to my eyes. It was all worth it and for the first time I could look up into the sky and feel the warmth of sunshine and imagine a future filled with hope and prosperity.

Everyone there was incredibly pleasant and caring. They offered me breakfast, but I couldn't eat yet. I felt like having something juicy instead of food, so I took few mandarins from my bag and ate that instead. One of the officers was especially kind and bought me some apples, oranges, and a sandwich. Around 10 that morning I was driven to a police station in a different town called Igoumenitsa. I was told that I had to spend the day there and in the evening I would be taken to Athens, the capital of Greece. It was a really boring stay at the police station that day.

I had a lot of time to think of the people I had left back home. I worried about the unknowns I would face in Greece. I was also excited about the promise for a brighter future as I turned my back on Albania. I didn't know how the lifestyle was in Greece; or how I would begin my new life; what I would do for my future in an entirely different country with a way of life for which I had no frame of reference. There were so many questions and thoughts racing through my mind with no answers.

I felt overwhelmed because life in Albania was all I had ever known. I started thinking about my family and the reality of what had happened to me in the past few days begun to sink in. I was missing them already and feeling guilty about how their lives would be impacted because of my escape. My calculations about the escape itself had led me to success, but I didn't know how accurate my predictions were concerning my family and what would happen to them.

I didn't even know how I would find out if something did happen to them. More than anything, I was anxious they would pay the price for my actions. It was difficult not to imagine my mother's anguish and how painful it would be for her to know that she had lost another child.

Over the years the system in Albania changed, but in the year of my escape neither escapee nor remaining family members expected to see each other again for the rest of our lives. My mother didn't know what had become of me—whether alive or dead—and no one knew how long it would take for her to find out. I knew for sure that nothing would ease my mother's pain.

I couldn't continue in this self-aggrandizing mood and eventually tried to think more positively. My mother would be peaceful to know that I was alive and well, and on the precipice of a better life. It would have been worse for her if I had been killed at the border.

These and other thoughts offered me little relief, and it became clear to me that thinking positive was a fleeting thought. I simply could not look beyond my past so quickly.

I couldn't explain the thoughts and feelings I had at the time. I was thrilled to be alive, but I couldn't ignore the emptiness I felt underneath my sense of accomplishment. The day in the office dragged on, but I was used to waiting by this time. Around 6 o'clock, two of the secret service men from the day before came to escort me to a camp in Athens. They did their best to explain what to expect. Our trip started by boarding a bus that was scheduled to leave around 8 o'clock that evening.

I could hardly contain my excitement once we were on the bus. I watched the streets spread out behind us as we drove, enthralled by the sights. I was so curious to see more of Greece. Everything was different compared to Albania.

The man whom I believed secretly spoke Albanian was sitting next to me. He was trying to have a conversation with me. I was looking outside and he asked me something in Greek. As I was looking out the window I thought he asked me what it was that I was looking at. I tried to answer him in Albanian, but it was impossible to understand each other while speaking two different languages. As he had done the night before, he nodded at a certain moment as if he understood me.

Perhaps he was just being polite and this was his attempt to make me feel comfortable. Based on his body language and my general sense that he understood more than he let on, I asked if he spoke Albanian. He said he did; from that moment on, we spoke Albanian with each other. He said that he understood everything I had said the night before and that I was honest, but the fact that my cousin is a Secretary of the Party Committee of Gjirokaster worried the Greeks.

They were convinced that I was an agent sent by the Albanian government. That was the moment that raised so many questions for them, which was why they kept asking me questions all night long. He said that all of the answers were correct, especially when they asked me regarding the place where I spent the last months of my service.

Personally, he'd trusted me from the moment I described what the chief looked like. He knew the chief and all the details of the army base very well. He said that sometimes an agent sent by a different government

knew the main information but not the details of their
cover. My knowledge convinced them that I wasn't sent
as an agent by Albania.

I asked him how he managed to get into our
army base, because it is impossible to get in unless you
had security clearance. He explained to me that once
when Albania and Greece had to sign some agreements,
he was permitted to enter the base. They had a big party
that night and he became friends with the chief. He said
that they even went hunting together along the border.
Despite being friends with the chief, he meant me no
harm. He was impressed with my honesty and said that I
was intelligent and brave. He wished me good luck in
Greece and assured me that I would be safe there.

I didn't know anything about the refugee camp
they were sending me to and I had no idea how long I
would stay there, but this conversation eased some of my
concerns. I had been under investigation all that time,
and knowing that they trusted me felt great and gave me
faith that I would be released in a short period of time.

When the bus arrived in Athens, a police vehicle
was waiting for us to transport us to police headquarters.
It was around 3 o'clock in the morning. As soon as we
arrived I signed some papers and given a place to sleep.

It was my sixth night without much sleep. This was where people were held in temporary custody. Rather than place me in the cells, they directed me to sleep in an office, which had a bed. After they made sure I was all set we shook hands and said goodbye to each other and I went to bed.

At 7 o'clock I heard footsteps coming in my direction. As I slept facing the wall I couldn't see who was coming, but he ran out screaming at the sight of me. I guess he called a law enforcement officer and asked him why I was there, because within a minute an officer came to my bed. He kept whispering to me and I thought he was asking me to get up. My knee was stiff again, but I complied as quickly as I could.

Then two officers came to take me and send me behind bars where the other people were. I saw a large cell with a small door and roughly thirty people in it. At that point, I didn't know they were in custody for validating the laws. When I first saw them walking back and forth I couldn't understand why they were behaving that way. The officers opened the door and tried to place me in there.

I grabbed the bars on both sides of the door and refused to go in. I kept telling them I didn't belong there and that it was simply a misunderstanding. I tried to explain that they had the wrong person.

Apparently, they knew what they were doing, but I didn't know that I had to be held in there temporarily until I was released by the police. I had never been told. I was panicking and did not want to be held in a cell. I was not a criminal. They tried to push me inside, but couldn't. I grasped those bars and held on tightly. They started laughing and called for help. Another officer came, but that didn't help because I refused to let go of the bars. Then five more officers came. I did my best to resist them, but they took my hands off the bars and pushed me inside.

I still had my bag with food that the gentlemen from Filat bought me. The knife I brought from Albania was still in my bag, which worried me, because I didn't want it within reach of my cellmates. I didn't know who they were; why they were under arrest; or what was on their minds. Gesturing as intelligibly as possible I called one of the officers to tell him to get my bag out of there.

He took it and left it right outside of the cell. Again, this worried me. I squeezed my hand through the bars and pushed the bag as far away as I could. Shortly after I was placed in the cell, I got bored and started

walking back and forth like everybody else. Then I
realized why those people were walking constantly. The
room was big, but not big enough for 30 people. It didn't
have chairs, beds, or anything. Some cellmates placed
newspapers on the floor to sit on. Some were even
sleeping on the floor.

An officer came by the bars to let us know it was
breakfast time. He went through the menu and listed all
the names of the foods; I didn't know which food was
which, so I didn't order anything. Instead of ordering
something in a language I didn't speak, I asked the
officer to bring my bag close to me. I got an apple from
it and ate it for breakfast.

Late that morning, a couple officers came and
called the names of two Albanians. I recognized their
names. A week before I escaped, a soccer team from
Shkodra (a city in northwestern Albania) had a game
scheduled in Malta. On the way back from Malta, they
stopped in Greece to spend the night. They were
scheduled to go back to Albania in the morning, but that
night the goalkeeper and one of the offense players
escaped from the hotel. They stayed in Greece and
applied to be political refugees. When the officers called
their names I looked around the room and tried to locate

them. I was enthusiastic to meet someone else who had escaped and happy for the opportunity to speak my native tongue, but the soccer players had already moved on.

They called my name and said "Lavrio". I didn't understand what that meant, but I said "Albania" in response, thinking they wanted to know where I was from. I later found out that Lavrio was my next destination, but at that moment they kept saying "Lavrio" and I kept saying "Albania". In retrospect, they must have thought that I was insane each time I replied "Albania" when they said "Lavrio". It was as if I was asking them to take me back to Albania.

They transported me and two other people on the bus, which was full of released prisoners. The ride to Lavrio was about 90 minutes. On the way there the other two refugees came next to me, speaking in Greek. The only word I understood was "Turkish", so I assumed they were from Turkey. I said "Albanian" and couldn't carry on a conversation with them beyond that. They understood that I didn't know how to speak Greek and kept quiet for the rest of the ride.

We arrived at the police station in Lavrio. After we signed some paperwork, some other officers arrived to pick us up. Right across from the police building were three buildings side-by-side. One building was for Turkish refugees; one for Kurdish refugees; and one for refugees from other countries. That was where they dropped me off.

One of the officers in the refugee shelter took me into a room with four beds. He ushered me to my bed and closet and provided me with a set of sheets and two blankets. Next, he took me on a tour around the shelter. The shelter had security 24/7, but it wasn't enclosed with fence or anything. I wasn't sure if I was free to go outside of the shelter's immediate area, or if I had to return by a certain time. There were many unanswered questions.

Looking at the surroundings, I assumed I was free to go anywhere during the day. I didn't know the protocol so after the tour I went back to my room and laid down just to be safe. Two of my roommates were from Yugoslavia and the other one was from Ethiopia. One of the Yugoslavian men tried to explain the guidelines to me, but I didn't understand him. The conversation wasn't going anywhere. Sometimes they became frustrated and displayed signs that they thought I was incompetent, but that didn't bother me because I was new to the country and didn't know how to speak Greek. I wasn't ashamed of myself, even though they tried to make me feel that way.

I stayed in bed for the rest of the day and didn't even go to the cafeteria for food. I ate what was left in my bag. The next morning, when I woke up I was in pain and my leg was stiff again. I went to see the refugee doctor in the shelter and she gave me a tube of cream to massage my knee. She never ordered an x-ray or any other exams. It was the cream and I was let go.

I was very disappointed with the doctor because she had done nothing to help me more than giving me a tube of cream. Although I was in severe pain I couldn't do anything because I didn't even know how to communicate with her. Up to this moment my language barrier had not posed a serious problem. But this was my health and I couldn't even communicate with the doctor to ensure that I receive the best possible care for my ailing knee. It took approximately six months for my knee to heal on its own.

I went back to my room and massaged my knee. Then I went to the cafeteria to get some food. That was the first time I walked freely along the streets of Greece. I went around the town and familiarized myself with the area. But the language barrier again proved to be a problem.

For nearly six months I had nightmares almost every night about my escape. I dreamt that I was back in Albania worried that the communists would arrest me for escaping the country. Then, I dreamt about whether I would be able to escape again and how to do it.

I woke up and saw that I was already in Greece and couldn't believe that I was there because of my nightmares. I was tormented by these nightmares at night and tried to live a normal life during the day. I was determined to learn the language and in a very short time made dramatic improvements. After a month or so I was approached by a tall, gray-haired man in his 60s who was also fluent in Albanian. After introducing himself Mr. G went on to explain how his family had escaped from Albania when he was very young.

He was the President of Syllogos, a Greek organization that supported the idea that southern Albania belonged to Greece. I remembered seeing him in Albania a few years before my escape, but I didn't know who he was at the time. A troupe of Greek singers came to perform in my town and he was the formal host. After introducing himself he promised he would help me if I went to Athens. He informed me that there was a hotel where other Albanian refugees were temporarily living. However, I was very suspicious about his offers. We spent almost half a day together, but I was still unsure about him.

Based on the way he behaved and the resources he was offering I sensed that he was a double agent. It was impossible for someone like him who escaped years ago, now president of an anti-Albanian organization, to return to Albania and host a concert. The Albanian government never allowed individuals like him to visit the country. From that moment on I strongly believed he was an agent sent to capture refugees.

I didn't trust him, but I had to play his game and act like he was fooling me. I needed to get as much information and assistance as I could. Ultimately, I planned to travel to the United State of America, so I needed to find out where and how to apply for a permanent resident status. Additionally, I needed to get to know more Albanian refugees in order to start a truly independent life in Greece. As he was leaving he gave me his office address in Athens and told me I could drop by anytime.

I didn't understand the purpose of his visit that day. Once he had gone I went to speak with the security officer at the shelter. Part of the conversation was done in sign language and part of it in Greek. But I was able to get my message across. I wanted to know who Mr. G was, as well as how he discovered me. I was worried: how did this stranger find out all about me in a very short time?

However, the security officer told me not to worry: I was safe for now. However, as a precaution I went only on to crowded places from that moment on. I didn't want to give Mr. G a chance to capture me and send me back to Albania.

After some time had passed I decided to go to his office in Athens with the hope of meeting other refugees. When I arrived there, Mr. G introduced me to Ben, who was from Tirana (the capital of Albania). Ben had escaped by sneaking onto one of the ships that traveled from Albania to Greece. I had a reassuring conversation with him, and before I said goodbye, I asked him for a favor: since I wasn't familiar with Athens I asked him if he could assist me with the visa process.

A month later we went to immigration together and I filled out an interview appointment form for the American Embassy and applied as a political refugee. Once I had finished my business with immigration, I went back to the shelter in Lavrio. While waiting to hear from the Embassy my roommate from Ethiopia helped me find a temporary job.

My job entailed taking care of a Greek family's backyard. The owner of the house was an elderly woman whose husband had passed away and whose son was ill. She had olive trees in her backyard and it was harvest time. The owner hired me because she couldn't handle the volume of work. I built retaining walls around the olive trees, gathered all the olives, and tended to anything else that needed to be done in her backyard.

After I finished that job I worked for a contractor. I was his only employee and he loved me. I worked very hard and he always seemed very satisfied with what I had done. Every day after work, he took me to his house for dinner with his family. After dinner I returned to the shelter in Lavrio. Him and his wife treated me like a son, and I am forever grateful for his incredible kindness.

On one particular morning we were scheduled to start working later than usual, so we stopped at a cafe for coffee. By this time it had been approximately six months since I had escaped. I really missed my family and it was beginning to weigh heavily on me. At that moment it happens that a song was playing on the radio about the power of a mother's love. It really impacted me and tears begun to well up in my eyes. I missed my mother, my brother, and my three little nephews greatly.

I began to sob as my boss tried to calm me down. He encouraged me to man up (because men aren't supposed to cry, or something to that effect), but I just could not help myself. All those months of holding back my emotions had finally become unbearable and it all burst out. I explained to him how much I missed my family, and how I tried to be strong all these months—only to be broken by a song. He told me he understood my feelings, but that it had been an hour since I started crying and I had to calm down. He tried to tell me that I was making a scene. However, no matter what he said, I couldn't stop crying.

I had such a pain; such a longing in my chest, and it wouldn't let up. When he realized that he couldn't get me to stop crying, he decided that we should cancel work that day. Visibly shaken by my grief, he took me to his daughter's house nearby. When we arrived he turned on the music and urged me to release my pain and sorrow there in private.

That day I cried for almost six hours. I think the realization that I would never see my family again truly hit me the hardest when the song first played on the radio. I felt intensely guilty for leaving them. I didn't know if the government would punish them as a result of my actions. I didn't know what would become of them. After crying for so long, I finally felt some relief. Of course, the pain remained, but it became a little more bearable. Yet, this pain never completely subsides, it's like a phantom pain.

The next day I resumed my normal routine. As time passed I became accustomed to communicating in Greek. One day an officer from the shelter approached me as I was returning from work. In an excited tone, he asked me who I really was. Apparently, he thought I was someone important that he wasn't aware of. For the director of the Greek secret service to come there himself and ask to speak to me was, for them, a very surprising action.

The officer informed me that the director waited for me for about eight hours, then he left. He told the officer he would come back another day, and to relay the message to me. I wasn't expecting anyone and had no idea what this officer was talking about, and who this individual was. However, I knew that I hadn't done anything wrong, so I wasn't too concerned.

Two weeks passed before the director returned, hoping to see me. That day, I was told that he waited for almost four hours before giving up. However, before leaving he gave the officer a phone number for me to call. He also left a note with a date, time, and place to meet. According to the note, I was to meet him at the bus station from Lavrio to Athens. I had no idea why he wanted to talk with me personally, but I couldn't refuse —he was the director of the secret services of Greece. My boss couldn't work without an assistant, so both of us took that day off.

I took the bus to Athens and I arrived around 7:30 in the morning. I didn't know who I was meeting, so I just stared cluelessly into the crowd. Soon, I saw three gentlemen in suits and dark glasses exit a parked van and approached me. They knew exactly who I was. As we talked, the van pulled up next to us and I was

instructed to get in. At this time, I became a little
nervous. The van had no windows and I was blindfolded.
We drove for about an hour. I had no idea where they
were going, or what their intentions were. However, they
didn't seem malevolent, and they even struck up some
perfunctory conversation to pass the time. A few minutes
before we arrived at the destination; they removed my
blindfolds.

At that moment, I looked through the windshield
and saw that we were in the middle of a forest. Rolling
through a forest road, I noticed a couple of buildings.
They stopped the van there and brought me into one of
the buildings. It was still early in the morning, so they
stopped by the cafeteria and offered me breakfast. As
soon as I was settled down with my breakfast, they got
up and left. I was alone until someone passed by the
cafeteria door, pretending like he wasn't aware of my
presence. Then, very dramatically, he turned around and
approached me. I noticed right away that he knew who I
was and why I was there.

The gentleman asked me about my name, age,
and nationality. Then he asked me about my hometown.
Based on the questions he was asking me, I could tell
that he was very familiar with Gjirokaster. His next

series of questions gave me the impression that he believed I was an Albanian spy. Up to that moment, I answered his questions cautiously.

I wanted my responses to lead him to another question that would confirm my suspicions that he had been in Gjirokaster. Getting tired of the games, I suddenly spoke in Albanian to him. I asked him to tell me his real name and where he was originally from. I expressed my distrust towards him, and told him I wouldn't cooperate unless he was sincere with me. Taken aback at first, he hesitated to speak for a bit. However, he soon revealed who he really was: an Albanian refugee. He had escaped a long time ago, and his hometown was Dervician (a village near Gjirokaster). Suddenly nostalgic, we continued our conversation. I noticed that during our conversation, he kept looking at his watch.

After a while, he told me that it was time to go to the other building, where the director would come and meet me. He brought me to the auditorium of the adjacent building, which was full of workers. When I entered the auditorium everyone stared at me. During my time there everyone asked sarcastically if I had met Mr. G yet. I still didn't know why I was there, and wasn't sure how they knew who Mr. G was. Upon inquiring about Mr. G I learned that he was trying to send refugees back to Albania. My hunch was correct!

That day, I discovered that Mr. G was the former director of the secret services of Greece. While having a conversation with some of the workers I heard footsteps coming from the hallway. Everyone in the auditorium stopped talking as a deafening silence ensued. Someone walked through the door and everyone stood up to salute him. It was the current director of Greece's secret services. After everyone was seated, he introduced himself to me and started asking questions. He asked me about the Albanian military—mostly about weapon details. He then ordered everyone, except me, to leave the room.

As soon as we were alone he asked me if I liked Greece. Of course, I replied, "Yes." Then he offered me a job in the secret services. I told him I couldn't accept his offer because my dream was to go to the United States, and I was waiting on my visa. He asked me not to rush on my answer, and assured me that he wouldn't use me against Albania. He advised me to think it over, and that we would meet again later.

My answer was final, but he kept refusing to accept it. In the meantime, I explained to him that I couldn't ask for another day off work. However, he kept insisting, and even offered to pay both me and my boss for any workday we missed on his account. He told me to follow the same steps I did that day to come back to this place and give him a more thoughtful answer.

A couple of weeks later, I followed his instructions and I went back. He asked me if I had changed my mind. He was visibly disappointed when I refused his offer again, and he demanded an answer why I didn't want to work for the secret services. I clarified that I just wanted to make an honest living and that I didn't want to sleep with a gun under my pillow. I came to Greece to live freely and enjoy life. After a year or so, I had comfortably adjusted to the language and the culture. He simply shrugged.

FINDING WHAT WAS LOST

"Health is an unselected gift; family is a treasure;
you don't know how fortunate you are until you
possess both."——Vladimir Gjini

One day, one of the officers in the shelter advised me that two new Albanian refugees had arrived from Gjirokaster. As soon as I heard their names I realized that we knew each other quite well. I was incredibly excited to see them because this was my first chance to receive some credible information about my family. The officer didn't know if my two countrymen were coming to our shelter, but I had already resolved within myself to meet them. I knew the only person who could help me with this would be Mr. G because he would be the first to have information on Albanian escapees.

The next morning, I went to Athens to meet him and obtain the information I needed. Thankfully, Mr. G didn't give me any trouble. On the contrary, he provided me the address to their hotel. Upon my arrival, they were ecstatic to see me. It is, after all, very difficult to start a new life in a place where everyone is a stranger. We had lunch together, and they talked about the escape. They were the third successful escape from my hometown. Fifteen years before my attempt, someone succeeded. Then I did. And now them.

I couldn't wait to hear about my family. They told me that my family was alright; the government didn't send my brother in prison nor did they relocate my family. My mother took my escape very hard, they said. It was extremely difficult for her to manage the loss of a second child. She didn't know if I was dead, or where I was. She knew, however, that she would never see me again: so in a sense, I was dead. My sister was still married, and I was glad to hear that my brother-in-law didn't divorce her on my account. He was a staunch communist, so the chances of that happening were actually quite high.

However, I was most concerned about my brother. They told me that he was doing fine now, but he had had an extremely difficult time initially. He was discharged from his job, and everyone discriminated against him. A lot of his friends and most of our relatives began to refuse to associate with him. Even many who didn't bear any hard feelings towards him still had to keep their distance - in order to protect themselves.

Almost every morning, the government had him report to the police station. For hours, they would interrogate him there. I was disturbed to hear how much my brother had to suffer, but I was grateful that they didn't take him away from his family or imprison him. They also informed me that my cousin, who was a Secretary of the Party Committee of Gjirokaster, lost her position because of me and had to pick up some small office job. I later learned that on one occasion, several neighbors banded together in retaliation. They threw rocks at my house and broke all the windows. They discriminated against my family, accusing them of being traitors, disloyal, betrayers, and other terrible names.

My family went through a lot of turmoil. For example, it was a custom to visit family and friends to wish them a Happy New Year. My brother and his eldest son went to visit his sister for New Year. The brother-in-law answered the door. As soon as he recognized my brother he immediately cursed him; calling him a criminal, unpatriotic, deceitful, and other disturbing names. He chased my brother away, making sure to let him know that none of our family members were welcome at the communist family's home because of my escape. They experienced significant suffering and grief, but I felt better knowing that they were surviving nonetheless.

Apparently, a few days after my escape, my brother went to the police station and reported me as missing. When I didn't return from Saranda, his first thought was that I escaped, but he couldn't be sure. The whole town voluntarily swept the entire area searching for me, thinking that I was possibly murdered. I learned that the search - which even extended down to the nearby river - went on for two weeks. Shortly afterward, the authorities found out that I had escaped.

One morning, at around 11 AM, the government official in charge of propaganda at the factory where I worked gathered all 1,200 employees - my sister among them - to hear the announcement. He called me a traitorous bastard and an enemy of the country. He wanted them to hate me, to revile my name.

When my sister heard the announcement, she passed out. She never knew how I felt about the system: my brother had kept her in the dark. My escape was national news, and a big shock for my town. Everyone believed I was dead up until that moment. I chuckled when I learned that I was top dinner conversation in my town for nearly six months. No one expected me, that quiet person who never really complained, to up and leave one day without a word.

That day, the law enforcement officers went to my house and questioned my brother and sister-in-law for hours. They even questioned my three nephews, who were eleven, seven, and five years old at the time. They wanted to find any reason they could to send my brother in prison. They searched the entire house, trying to determine if I had any outside contact. Before I left the country, however, I destroyed all evidence of my escape. They confiscated a lot of pictures of me with my friends - they would end up questioning them all.

After telling me what they knew about my family, my friends asked me how I escaped. I briefly gave them an account of my escape, and how I meticulously planned every step in advance. I spent the whole day with my friends and got all the information I had been longing to hear for a year. I spent the night in their hotel room, and the next morning we went to visit some of my other friends in Athens.

I wanted to help these new arrivals find jobs and a new place to live. Living in that hotel for long was too dangerous for them - I knew it was one of the places where Mr. G and his crew tried to capture refugees and send them back to Albania. Ben (from Tirana) told me that during his second day in that hotel, three large men tried to capture him - fortunately, he was in a crowded area and managed to escape by yelling for help. One of my friends was kind enough to let them live in his apartment until they found their own. He even promised me he would help find jobs for them. The next day, I went back to Lavrio and back to work.

Having learned that my family was alright, it felt as if a huge weight had been lifted off my shoulders. Now, I just wanted to figure out a way to let them know that I was alive and doing well; however, I couldn't come up with a feasible plan.

One day, after I returned from work, one of my Yugoslavian roommates informed me about a trailer with Albanian license plates. He saw the trailer on a street near our area. I was very excited to hear this news, and I resolved to find it. Normally, the trailers parked at the port to load or unload goods. I took a quick shower, and my friend and I headed to the direction of the port. There, we saw the Albanian trailer parked. That evening, however, I was really looking for the driver - who wasn't in the trailer. As we walked down the boardwalk, I intentionally glimpsed at the shoes of the passersby. I had worked in a shoe factory long enough to immediately recognize Albanian styles and materials.

After a few minutes, I recognized two individuals in Albanian-style shoes. I didn't have the courage to stop them, so we followed them for a while. They stopped in a restaurant to have a dinner. I knew one of the cooks at that restaurant, so I went to the back (where the kitchen was) and asked him for a favor.

I wanted him to confirm through the waitress if those two individuals knew how to speak Greek, or if they spoke with an accent. He agreed. When the waitress came back, she informed us that they didn't know how to speak Greek. Upon hearing this, I went and sat at a table at the front of the restaurant with my friend.

I knew that drivers like them weren't allowed to have contact with anyone when they were outside Albania. If they were caught doing so, they could lose their job or even get sent to prison. I didn't want to harm them, so I watched what I said. After thinking for a moment, I turned around and said "hello" to them in Albanian. I could see they were shocked, but I introduced myself and assured them that I wasn't trying to harm them.

I explained to them that I was simply an escapee who wanted to talk with them for a few moments. They seemed okay with that, so I asked them which town they were from and if any of their routes took them through Gjirokaster. As it turns out, one of them was originally from Gjirokaster: he knew one of the supervisors of the factory I worked at. That supervisor happened to be the supervisor of the department in which I had worked. I was excited to hear that - he had an incredible personality, and he had always trusted me. I knew if he received a message from me, he would gladly pass it on to my family.

I asked the driver to, at his convenience, notify my former supervisor that I was alive and well in Greece. He agreed he would pass on the message. Ecstatic, I thanked them and told them that the dinner was on me. After dinner, I had planned to leave: I didn't want to cause them any trouble. However, they felt comfortable with me and Yugoslavian friend, so we went for a walk. They explained to me that they would be in Greece another night, so the next day we met for dinner. I made sure I showed my appreciation to them again.

I continued to work in construction at the time. The company did well until my boss started having gambling problems. He wasn't paying me consistently anymore, so I decided to terminate my employment with him and move to Athens. Initially, life was tough, but I eventually found a job that I enjoyed. I worked in a warehouse in Rafina, selling construction supplies. The owner worked the register until 1 PM, after which his father-in-law and I took over for the rest of the day.

The owner instructed me that if an order exceeded ten thousand drachma, I was to take the money out of the register and hide it on the nearby shelf. Thus, every time I received a big order, I hid the money and informed the owner the next morning. One afternoon, after a large transaction, as is typical, I hid the money in its usual spot. I was very busy the next morning, so I forgot to tell the owner about it. I noticed that he and his father-in-law were very angry all day, going in and out of the warehouse, but never saying anything to me. I knew something took place, but didn't ask: I thought it might've been a personal matter.

Later that afternoon, the father-in-law came in with his granddaughter. She was only five years old, and we had met before. As soon as she came in, she wanted to talk and play with me. All of a sudden, however, she asked me why her father wanted to send me back to

Albania. I had no idea why she said that, but I assured her he was just joking.

I had a great relationship with the owner, so I couldn't think of why he would want to do that. The next day, however, when the father-in-law and I were alone, he asked me if I had received a big order a couple of days ago. I told him that we had, and showed him where the money was, explaining why it was there instead of the register. He yelled at me, ordering me to never do that again. At that moment, I understood what had been going on. The following morning, the owner came and apologized for his father-in-law's behavior.

While I very much enjoyed my life in Greece, I didn't like one aspect of their culture: if you weren't Greek, you were always treated as a stranger and a refugee. My dream was to live in the United States of America, which had always been, in my mind, the greatest country in the world.

One day, I received a letter from the American Embassy—stating that I was approved to be a permanent resident of the United States. Elated, I went to the Embassy to start the visa process. I filled out all the documents, sat through all the interviews, and completed my visa. Finally, I knew the date I would arrive at the

United States. It took around a year and a half to complete the process.

FREEDOM I ONCE ONLY DREAMED OF

"Freedom is never dear at any price. It is the breath of life. What would a man not pay for living?"—
Mahatma Gandhi

In September 1989, my dream became a reality. That month I received a ticket to fly to the United States at JFK airport in New York. I had a window seat, and just before the flight landed, I got to see New York for the first time.

It was a beautiful afternoon, and I couldn't believe my eyes. It was breathtaking to see all the buildings, highways, and cars. At the same time, it was almost disorienting to see the vehicles travel in many different directions. For a moment, I didn't think I would ever be able to drive on those streets. I became very emotional, seeing with my own eyes what I had only dreamed of.

There were about 1,600 immigrant arrivals that day, and I had to go through immigration to receive my green card. Afterwards, I was scheduled to get on another flight to Seattle, Washington. For reasons I can't explain many of us missed the connecting flight that day, and I had to stay in a hotel for the night. The next morning, I flew to Chicago (where I had a layover), and from there to Seattle. When I arrived in Seattle that evening, I met my sponsor for the first time. He was waiting for me, holding a sign with my name. It was extremely difficult for me. I didn't know how to speak any English.

Thankfully, my sponsor was a wonderful man, incredibly kind and polite. He rented a small apartment for me and took me there. He showed me around and, as he was leaving, left me his phone number for whenever I needed him. Soon after arriving in the United States, I began receiving food stamps. I was moved. I had just arrived to this country, and the government provided me with the basic necessities. I couldn't believe that I, a refugee, mattered to them.

Of course, I still had a challenging time adjusting. I was in a new country with its own culture and foreign language. Although I practiced English every day and was determined to find a job, it didn't make things any easier for me. For example, while I was fortunate to receive food stamps, I still didn't know how to acquire the food I was entitled to. And, since I hadn't learned to speak or read English as yet, the street signs were of no help when it was time for me to navigate the community in search of grocery stores.

My sponsor tried to help me, but it was extremely difficult to communicate with him since I didn't speak English. After four months in Seattle, I still hadn't met another Albanian or Greek. For months, I didn't speak to anyone. Every day, however, I stood in front of the mirror and talked to myself for about five minutes to keep my vocal chords active. I was very concerned that I'd lose my voice if I didn't use it regularly in some type of conversation.

Truthfully, I didn't have many job opportunities there. After giving it some thought, I decided to move to the Northeast where I heard that many Albanians and Greeks lived. When I lived in Greece, I heard that Greeks owned most of the diners in the area.

Shortly after moving there, I found a job at a diner as a dishwasher. The owner of the diner was Greek, and we were able to communicate with ease. Starting from the ground up as a dishwasher I learned many aspects of the business which enabled me to become a cook. I worked as a cook for about nine years. Later, I transitioned to a limousine driver.

After living in the United States for five years, I became a citizen. In 1996, I married an amazing Albanian woman named Anila. In 1998, I became a father, and was blessed with a gorgeous little girl named Erisa. In 2003, we had a second child, a precious baby boy named Albi which he made me feel complete. Finally, I had built a family with whom I could enjoy life like never before. Every time I close my eyes to sleep I feel at peace knowing that my wife and children are healthy, happy, safe, and all their needs are met. What more could a person want? That's why I feel so blessed.

Currently, I live in Bergen County, New Jersey, and I own a house (which is, in my mind, the American Dream). My wife and I are very happy, and we can both wholeheartedly say that we love this country. I know what it is like to live under the bonds of tyranny and oppression. It is a miserable existence.

In 1991, Albania's communist system collapsed. It was probably one of the best events that could have occurred. This meant that I would have the opportunity to return to the country of my birth to see, touch, and cry for joy with my family again. With the fall of Communism in Albania it also meant that all the peril, pain, and despair that I endured was not in vain. There was no secret that all my family, friends, and neighbors, including me, knew that we would never see each other again. Thank God we were all wrong!

Following the great news of the end of communism I still proceeded with caution, not wanting to take any chances. I couldn't trust the former system and I was uncertain if I would be prevented from returning to America, or if I would be penalized for escaping years ago. These fears were real, and they were stronger than my deep longing to return to Albania, especially to see my mother. As a result, I waited three years to make sure that individuals who went to visit Albania from America were able to return to the States safely.

In 1994, I decided it was time to return to Albania and visit my family. Everyone was thrilled to hear the news. My best friend, Namik, said that he would be the one to pick me up from Mother Teresa Airport in Tirana. Although it was an expensive commitment for him, I will forever remember his kind gesture and commitment to our friendship to be there for me. However, when I arrived in Tirana he did not come alone. My brother and other family members were with him as well. Everyone wanted to enjoy that moment that they never thought would ever occur.

It was around 1:20 AM when I arrived in my hometown Gjirokaster. When we were about 1,000 feet from my house, Namik sounded the horn three times to announce my arrival. As we approached the house I saw an enormous crowd waiting for me outside. Even though it was very dark and packed with people, I was still able to recognize my mother waiting anxiously to reunite with her son, whom she never expected to see again. Reuniting with my mother was by far one of the most emotional and memorable moments of my life.

Here I am reuniting with my mother for the first time since escaping from communist Albania. It was the highlight of an emotional experience.

The excitement and emotions of those moments were indescribable. One memory that is engraved into my mind forever was when my youngest nephew, Jonuz, grabbed me from my pants and tried to draw my attention. The crowd was too big and he was concerned that I forgot about him. Jonuz wanted a hug and a kiss. As far as he was concerned I had withheld my attention from him long enough, and he couldn't wait any longer. After I greeted everyone we went inside and celebrated until the next morning. We all experienced an overpowering sense of peace and euphoria.

My brother provided everything for the celebration, but I was astonished by one of my neighbor's action. He was extremely poor, yet as soon as we went inside he went back to his house for a while. No one knew the reason for his disappearance until he returned with a whole roasted lamb. That was the only lamb that he owned, but he was generous, overjoyed, and thought nothing of his own economic situation.

During my stay there I tried to spend as much time as I could with my mother, but it seemed that what little time we shared could never be enough.

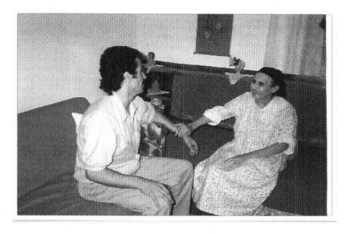

Here I am catching up with mom after a very long time apart.

As my days in Albania quickly passed it was time to return to my home in America. In America, I work hard, yet I still find time every day to enjoy as much of the incredible freedom that we have—a freedom I once only dreamed of.

ABOUT THE AUTHOR

Vladimir Gjini was born in 1962 in Gjirokaster, Albania, where he spent the first 25 years of his life. In Revealing the Untold: My Courageous Journey and Escape from Extreme Oppression, Vladimir shares how he overcame extreme suffering and hardship. Despite the communist regime, he made his way to America in 1989, where he has lived ever since.

Vladimir is the owner of Rainbow Limousine, an executive transportation company. He began his career in the limousine industry in 1998. His warm personality, welcoming smile and enthusiasm help to deliver superior customer service to his clients. Excellence and success is shown through his passion and his dedication.

The biggest influence on Vladimir's life has been his family. His life's purpose is to give his children what he was deprived of in his childhood.